Angel

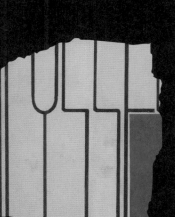

, erotic nove

SHOGUN
NOVEL OF JAPAN

...GRIPPING.
NEW YORK TIMES

The Mea
of Beaut

Eric Newton

adame

ulie

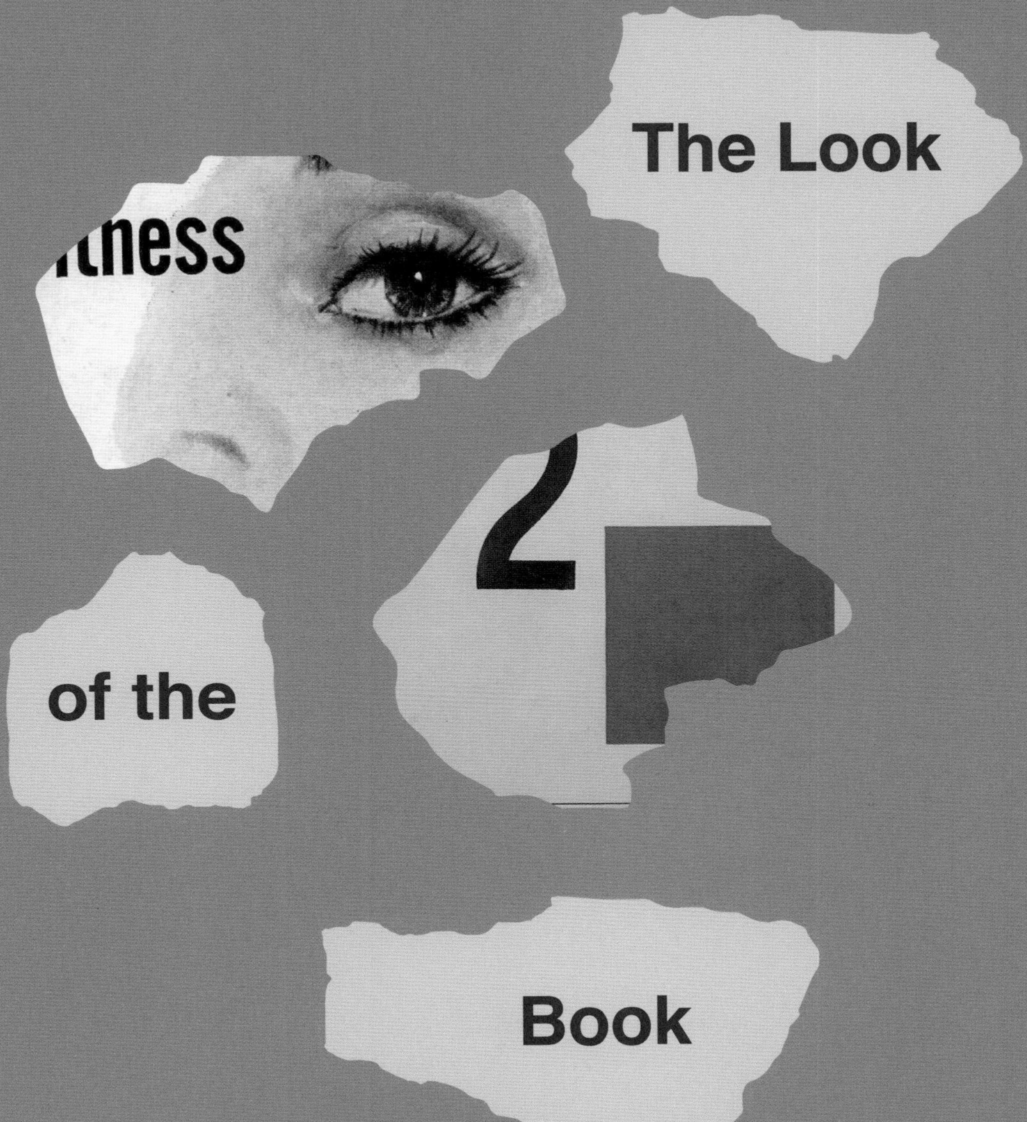

tness

The Look

of the

2

Book

The Look

UOM

se-pounding thriller with echoes of
—*Publishers Weekly*

of the

Book

OF
SPACE

Jackets,
Covers & Art
at the Edges of
Literature

H. P.
AND AUG
STORIES OF A MASTER
THE SUN
AND OTH

ONRAK

Peter
Mendelsund

David J.
Alworth

Blo
Trum

TEN SPEED PRESS
California | New York

Preface

Meeting at the Edge

Portnoy's Complaint
Philip Roth

Book covers ...

A Fawcett Crest Book

P1313
$1.25

3 Months on The New York Times bestseller list

The Tin Drum

Günter Grass

"One of the greatest literary adventures of our time"

READ

You Shall Know Them
A novel by VERCORS

The extraordinary story of a man who deliberately
committed murder (but was it murder?) to test a
question that touches every human being.

THIS

just about anything
to get noticed.

They will flirt ...

Goodbye, Columbus

and 5 short stories

by Philip Roth

Meridian Fiction MF5 $1.45 / Canada $1.60

Paul Rand

shimmy,

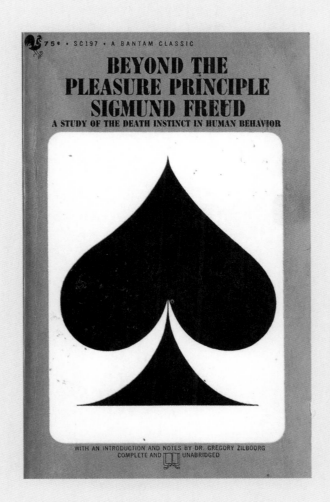

wink,

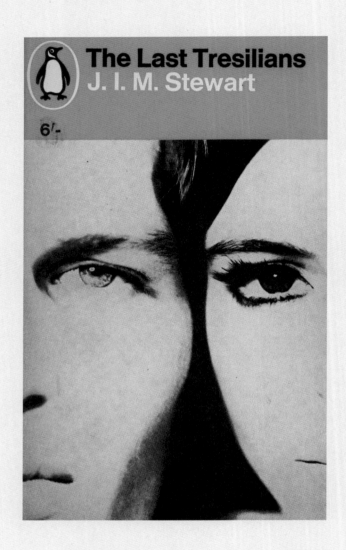

The Last Tresilians

J. I. M. Stewart

6/-

stare,

shout,

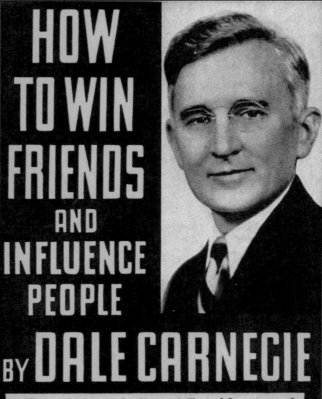

make promises,

or break the fourth wall.

They might frighten

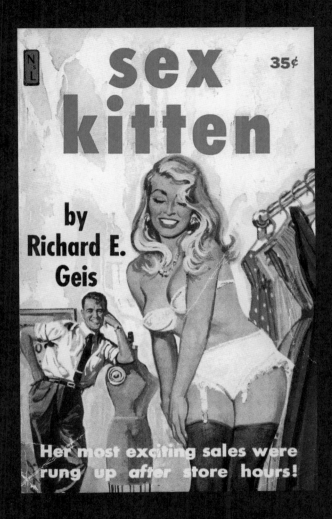

sex kitten

35¢

by Richard E. Geis

Her most exciting sales were rung up after store hours!

or titillate,

obfuscate

a Pelican Book

Self
and Others
R. D. Laing

or illustrate,

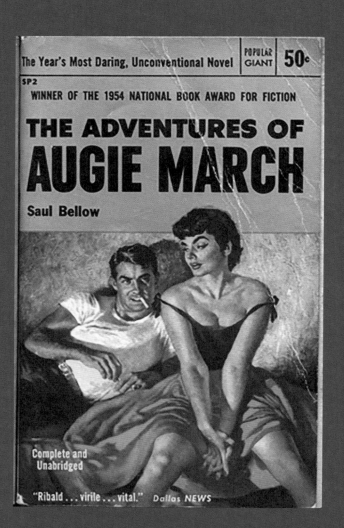

The Year's Most Daring, Unconventional Novel

POPULAR GIANT

50¢

SP2

WINNER OF THE 1954 NATIONAL BOOK AWARD FOR FICTION

THE ADVENTURES OF AUGIE MARCH

Saul Bellow

Complete and
Unabridged

"Ribald...virile...vital." Dallas NEWS

introduce characters

or obscure them,

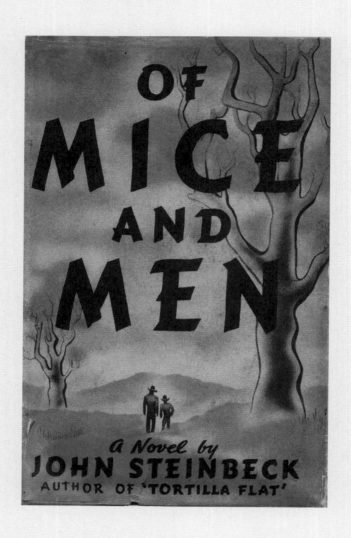

set the stage

or set the mood,

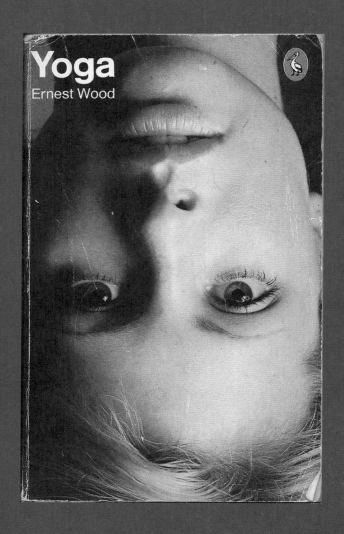

Yoga

Ernest Wood

change your perspective

"Fascinating and disturbing, amusing and informative, Faster is an eclectic stew combining history, academic research, and anecdotes drawn from the popular media." —The Boston Globe

FSTR

FASTER THE ACCELERATION
OF JUST ABOUT EVERYTHING

JMS

JAMES GLEICK author of GENIUS

GLCK

or save you time.

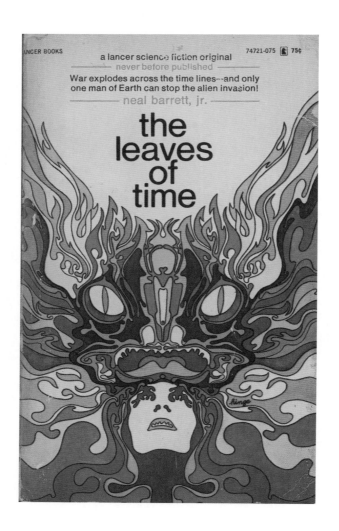

the leaves of time

They can be colorful

or not.

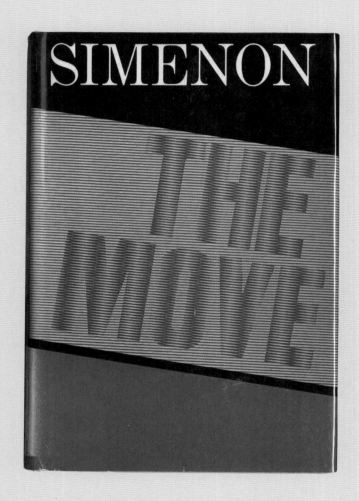

They may vibrate

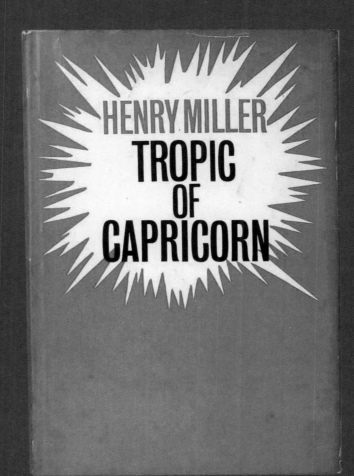

or explode.

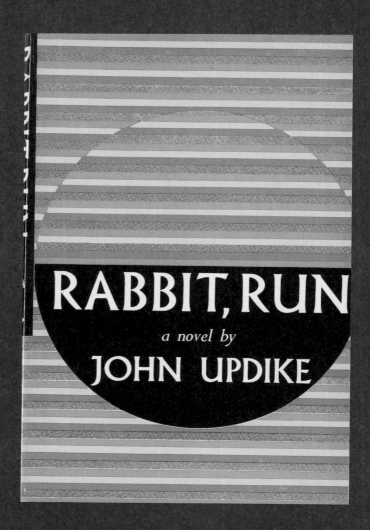

They may be decorative

THE NEW TESTAMENT

translated by

RICHMOND LATTIMORE

or challenging.

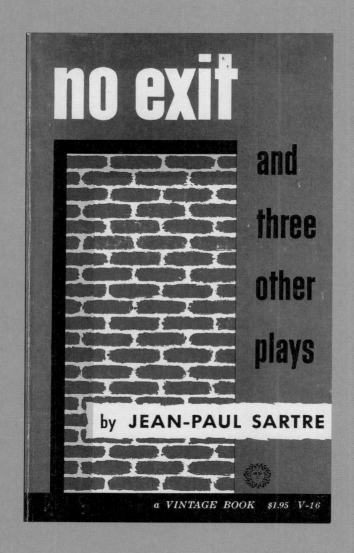

no exit

and

three

other

plays

by JEAN-PAUL SARTRE

a VINTAGE BOOK $1.95 V-16

They can be literal

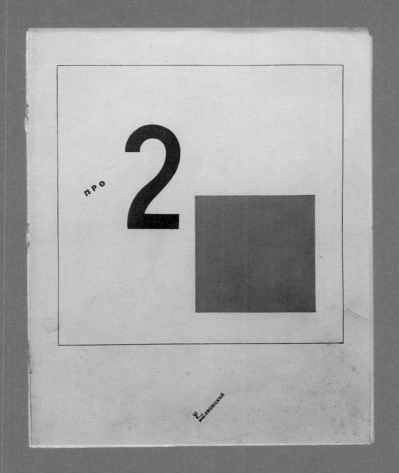

or abstract,

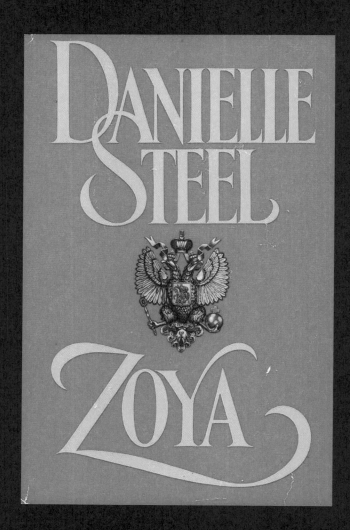

commercial

The Psychology
of Communication
Seven Essays
George A. Miller

or academic,

COMPASS

MATHIAS ENARD

Fitzcarraldo Editions

generic

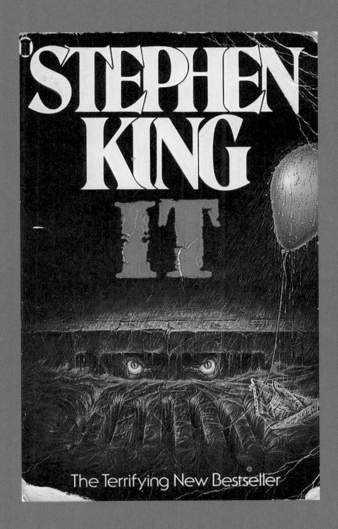

or genre specific.

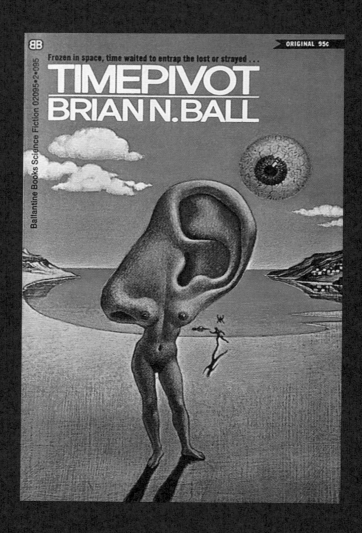

They may be intentionally confusing

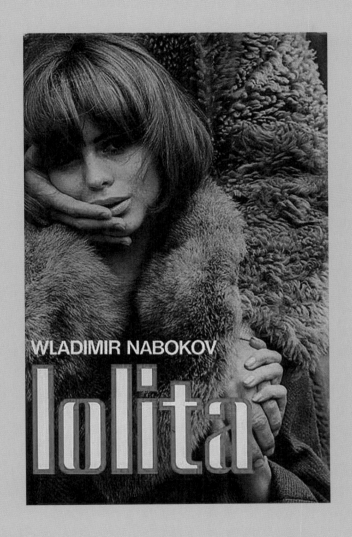

or unintentionally confusing.

Some book covers are bespoke;

others are boilerplate.

Some tell us about the text;

others tell us almost nothing at all.

As readers and
consumers,
we're all familiar
with the
pleasures and
pitfalls of

judging a book
by its cover.

We're not supposed to do it, but we do it anyway. The book cover is the outward face of the text, the all-important first impression of the text, but it's also incidental and easily replaced. The same text can take many different covers without losing its identity.

These contradictions started to intrigue us the more we thought about them. Eventually, they got us thinking about the book cover as a specific medium of communication, graphic expression, design, and perhaps even art. There really is no other medium quite like it, but as is the case with all media in the twenty-first century, the book cover is being transformed by the digital revolution. Until recently, talking about book covers meant talking about physical books: either hardbacks (with or without paper jackets) or paperbacks. In the era of e-books and audiobooks, however, book covers exist as digital images that can float free of the texts that they cover. These days, we are likely to see a new book in the form of a publicity image before we can purchase it. As visual designs, book covers must accomplish a nearly impossible task: they have to be as effective at 1½ inches tall, which is the size of an Amazon thumbnail image, as they are at 9 inches tall, displayed in the window of the brick-and-mortar bookstore. For this reason and others, the look of the book matters now as never before.

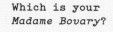

Which is your
Madame Bovary?

WDL BOOKS

GUSTAVE FLAUBERT'S

Immortal

Madame Bovary

A BRILLIANT AND CYNICAL STORY OF THE WOMAN WHO FLOUTED THE MORAL LAWS OF HER DAY

3'6

COMPLETE AND UNABRIDGED

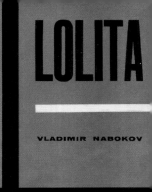
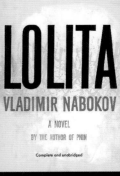

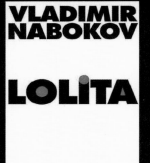

The book cover provides a concrete example of text meeting context.

And which is
your *Lolita*?

What is the status of the book cover in the twenty-first century? In the pages that follow, we approach this question from multiple angles, though our emphasis falls on book design for literary fiction. This is what we mean by *art at the edges of literature*. We are especially interested in what happens when literary texts prompt visual designs—in the way that texts, through the cover-design process, give rise to icons, images, figures, and compositions in another medium.

To transform a manuscript into a bona fide book is to create a visual and tangible thing through a process that involves many people, all of whom are grappling with the question of how to present a new book to the world. It is a question not of judging but of nudging a book by its cover. The book cover provides a concrete example of text meeting context, for it is a site where literature intersects with visual culture, business, politics, law, and even history. Examining the book cover allows us to glimpse the connection between an individual author's vision and the social, cultural, and historical circumstances of the time (or multiple times, as when the same text is re-covered with the publication of each new edition).

Every book cover, moreover, provides an interpretation of the text at hand. The book cover represents the designer's (or the design team's) reading of the manuscript, and as with all readings, it responds not only to the text but also to the pressure of the world: the imperative to sell books, to please the boss, to appease the author, to avoid cliché, to make a notable design. Does this mean that book covers are merely marketing tools? We don't think so. We even think that they can attain the status of art, although this claim will require some explaining on our part, since art is usually understood to have no commercial purpose whatsoever, and there's no getting around the fact that book covers are advertisements. Like a bag of potato chips or a television commercial, book covers have an obvious mandate, which is to sell a commodity, except in the case of literature the commodity is also art.

This book is an experiment in thinking and writing between the disciplines of literary theory and design. We're two friends who work in different areas of contemporary book culture, but we share multiple interests: modern art, the history of the novel, philosophy, and media theory. As we worked on this book together and discovered the power of collaboration, we came to realize that designers and writers have much to discuss. Still, it can be difficult to initiate and sustain a dialogue across the verbal-visual divide, partly because of the longstanding convention in publishing that places authors and designers in separate silos. As we interviewed people for this book, many writers, critics, and scholars told us that they were discouraged from talking extensively with their cover designers. There might be a good reason for this: cover designers are professionals with a genius for visual communication, and they need to be able to work without too much meddling from outside parties. Even the most visually minded authors might not have the best ideas for how to cover their book, just as the most sophisticated designer might not be able to write lively prose. At its best, however, the cover-design process engages different people with distinct talents to turn a manuscript into something more: a fully formed book, a work of art, a delightfully designed commodity, a lasting contribution to knowledge or culture. And this process, as we try to show throughout this book, prompts lots of interesting questions that deserve consideration from all.

The idea for *The Look of the Book* came about after we taught a college class together, in which the students were tasked with designing new book covers for the novels on a syllabus that included Vladimir Nabokov, Thomas Pynchon, Gertrude Stein, and James Baldwin. Some students were brave enough to work on *Gravity's Rainbow*, an encyclopedic novel that conveys an enormous amount of visual detail. Others tried their hand at *Lolita*, taking on an extraordinary ethical challenge. All of them worked hard. And their remarkable designs—mostly hand-drawn illustrations on quality paper stock with some tooth—convinced us to explore the meaning and value of the book cover in a time when we hear so much about the death of the physical book.

Like a bag of potato chips or a television commercial, book covers have an obvious mandate, which is to sell a commodity, except in the case of literature the commodity is also art.

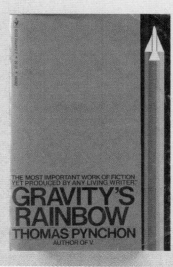

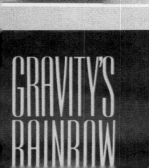

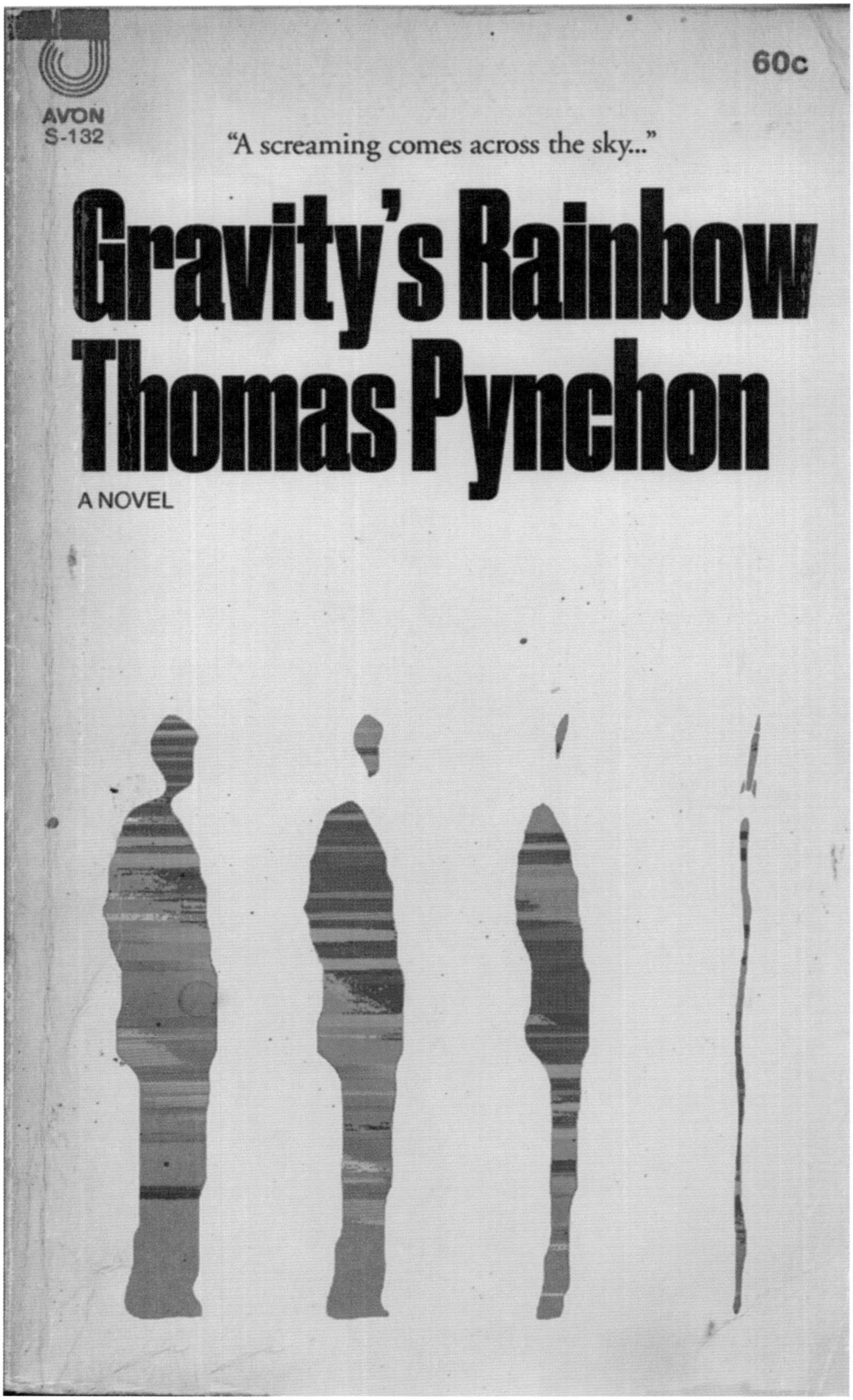

AVON
S-132

60c

"A screaming comes across the sky..."

Gravity's Rainbow
Thomas Pynchon

A NOVEL

Unused cover comp of *Gravity's Rainbow* by Thomas Pynchon, design by Peter Mendelsund: Slothrop's gradual decline into disorder, deliquescing into a V-2 rocket.

Our students, digital natives, were allowed to submit TIFFs or JPEGs or PDFs, but most chose to design covers the old-fashioned way: sketching by hand, cutting with scissors, pasting with paste. It was a reminder that the physical book, and the craft associated with book design, will not simply disappear as Kindle and Audible editions become more prevalent in the classroom and elsewhere. Indeed, even though e-books are convenient and audiobooks are conducive to multitasking, the physical book, and specifically the codex or paged book, retains a certain allure. At the same time, though, there is no denying that Amazon (and digitization in general) has radically altered the technological and social conditions for book-cover design. We are living through a media revolution whose outcome is uncertain.

The Look of the Book, then, is an effort to take stock of where we are, where we have been, and where we might go as readers and book lovers. Combining the insights of literary theory and design, we explore what the book cover is, what it was, what it does, and why it matters. As collaborators striving to overcome the limitations of our respective professional fields, we put words and images in conversation with one another, and this book is meant to be both read and looked at simultaneously. We pull back the curtain on the design process, showing how covers get made, which involves talking about sketches, iterations, failures, revisions, thrilling approvals, and heartbreaking rejections. And while we emphasize the viewpoint of the reader, we also let writers have their say, since few experiences in a writer's life are more delicate than the experience of delivering a manuscript to those who will decide how it should appear in the world.

Still, some of our predilections remain. Heavily weighted toward books written in English and toward traditional publishing in the United States, this book is not a comprehensive account of cover design across the globe, nor is it a complete history of the tropes, trends, and styles of book art. We began with the material that we knew best—book design for contemporary literary fiction—and found that there was a lot to say about it. Instead of a broad survey of book covers, many of which already exist, we wanted to offer an extended consideration of the most interesting questions that emerge during the multiphase process that turns manuscripts into books. Our past experiences and research methods shaped the stories, claims, and case studies that follow. We conducted interviews and assembled oral histories, did image research, and studied previous scholarship in media studies, literary theory, and book history. We gave talks on this project and fielded questions that prompted additional research and thinking. Some of the work that we discuss comes from our personal archives, some from the public domain. We have tried to be diligent, but our methods are imperfect and idiosyncratic. There will be important covers and designers we have missed.

We hope, nonetheless, that this book will provide a new perspective on the old medium of the book cover. If *The Look of the Book* prompts future research and writing on the topic, we will be very pleased, even if such research makes the limitations of our work seem all the more glaring. Based on in-depth interviews with authors and designers, the concluding chapter, "Conversations at the Edge," is meant to stimulate fresh discussion about the cover-design process. A glossary at the end of the book defines technical terms. We're glad that you've met us here, at the intersection of writing and design, to explore art at the edges of literature.

"The dates for the earliest printed book jackets, or as they're now called, dust jackets, are impossible to pinpoint. Scholars, booksellers, and collectors have been endeavoring to identify the earliest jacket for two or three generations, since the moment when the market began to place a premium on first editions that survived wrapped in their original jackets. In my decades of dealing books I've never encountered a pre-twentieth century jacket that suggested any purpose beyond either protecting the book beneath it or to offer a modest decorative element to the object being offered for sale. It strikes me that both of those impulses are commercial: to make the exchange of the book for cash a clean and pleasant experience. If I'm right, then the leap into the twentieth century and the creation of jackets that serve as a form of advertising was a logical and utilitarian progression. After the first World War, as the market grew more crowded with trade books and literacy increased dramatically, publishers needed fresh ways to distinguish their wares from those of their competitors. A compelling question that this observation raises is whether there really was a relationship between the pictorial images now regularly decorating the front of jackets and the texts of the books those jackets were wrapped around."

—Glenn Horowitz, bookseller

1.

What the Book Cover Is

The Book Jacket

1. Blurbs 2. Author Photo and Bio
3. Design, Art, and Photo Credits 4. Publishing Info 5. Barcode

1.

BACK FLAP   BACK OF JACKET

2.

MATHIAS ÉNARD is the
award-winning author of *Zone* and
Street of Thieves and a translator
from Persian and Arabic. He won
the Prix Goncourt in 2015 for *Compass*.

CHARLOTTE MANDELL has
translated works by a number of important
French authors, including Proust, Flaubert,
Genet, Maupassant, and Blanchot.

Design by Peter Mendelsund

NEW DIRECTIONS
INDEPENDENT PUBLISHER
SINCE 1936
80 EIGHTH AVENUE
NEW YORK 10011

3.

4.

"This astonishing, encyclopedic, and otherwise ou-
tré meditation by Énard on the cultural intersection
of East and West takes the form of an insomniac's
obsessive imaginings—dreams, memories, and desires—which come to embody the content of a life, or
perhaps several. An opium addict's dream of a novel."
—*Publishers Weekly*

"Mathias Énard has found a way to restore death to life
and life to death, and so joins the first rank of novelists, the bringers of fire, who even as they can't go
on, do."—Garth Risk Hallberg, *The Millions*

"Mathias Énard is the most brazen French
writer since Houellebecq."—*New Statesman*

"Compass is a profound and subtle tale. Énard is an
immensely ambitious writer—luckily, his ambition is
matched by his equally extraordinary talent."
—Alberto Manguel, *El País*

"I'm grateful to Mathias Énard for having given me
the chance to read about an Orient that includes as
much complexity as humanity. It's not the Orient of
the Other, but a reader's and a writer's experience. If I
dared, I would say that it's a participatory Orient."
—Kamel Daoud, author of *The Meursault Investigation*

NDBOOKS.COM

5.

6. Main Typography: Title, Author, Reading Line, and Cover Quote 7. Teaser
8. Price 9. Colophon 10. Cover Image 11. Synopsis and Publisher Statement

6.

7.

SPINE · FRONT OF JACKET · FRONT FLAP

COMPASS

MATHIAS ÉNARD

Winner of the Prix Goncourt

FICTION · USA $26.95
CAN $35.95

Translated by Charlotte Mandell

As night falls over Vienna, Franz Ritter, an insomniac musicologist, takes to his bed with an unspecified illness and spends a restless night drifting between dreams and memories, revisiting an ongoing fascination with the Middle East and his numerous travels to Istanbul, Aleppo, Damascus, and Tehran, as well as the various writers, artists, musicians, academics, translators, orientalists, and explorers who populate this vast dreamscape. At the center of these memories is Sarah, a fiercely intelligent French scholar caught in the intricate tension between Europe and the Middle East.

With exhilarating prose and sweeping erudition, Mathias Énard pulls astonishing elements from disparate sources—nineteenth-century composers and esoteric orientalists, Balzac and Proust, Thomas Mann and Sadegh Hedayat—and binds them together in a hypnotic, magical way, as a powerful ode to Otherness.

A NEW DIRECTIONS BOOK

8.

9.

10.

11.

A book cover

is not one
thing.

It is, in fact,

multiple
things.

As a physical component of the book, the cover is a skin, a membrane, and a safeguard: paper jackets protect hardback boards from scuffing and sun damage, while paperback covers not only hold the book together but also keep its sheets clean and safe from tearing. In the past, paper jackets were plain wrappers used to shield decorative bindings, but around the turn of the twentieth century, illustration migrated from the boards to the jackets themselves (see chapter two). In a metaphorical sense, a book cover is also a frame around the text and a bridge between text and world. The cover functions simultaneously as an invitation to potential readers and as an entryway into the universe that the writer has created, whether fictional, historical, autobiographical, or otherwise. Come, it says, join the party—or at least save the date.

As a designed object, the book cover is a first look at the text and a visual rendering of what the text says: it is both an interpretation and a translation from verbal into visual signifiers. While the cover designer may wish to convey something original,

there are constraints on the design process, since the book cover also serves as a kind of information kiosk that not only indicates author, title, and publisher but also locates the book in relation to genre. There are well-established visual tropes for genres such as crime, science fiction, fantasy, and romance, but all books must announce their place with respect to other books. No one likes false advertising.

Books also need to sell themselves, so covers can be understood as teasers, functioning much like movie trailers, giving us just enough detail—including comments from other readers, known as "blurb" writers, whose praise is in fact promotion—to entice us to buy the book. The blurb is a standard feature of many book covers, but for nearly as long as it has been around, it has provoked suspicion, ridicule, and even scorn. George Orwell, in 1936, blamed the novel's decline on "the disgusting tripe that is written by the blurb-reviewers."[1] Camille Paglia called blurbs "absolutely appalling" in a 1991 speech.[2] This antiblurb tradition stretches all the way back to the inventor of the term, Gelett

Gelett Burgess coined the term "blurb" to parody a convention that was becoming more widespread in book publishing during the early twentieth century.

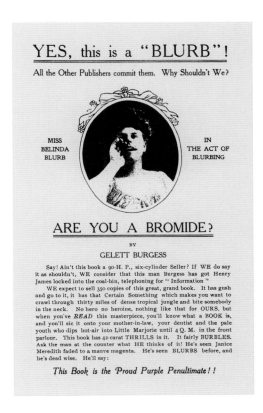

YES, this is a "BLURB"!

All the Other Publishers commit them. Why Shouldn't We?

MISS
BELINDA
BLURB

IN
THE ACT OF
BLURBING

ARE YOU A BROMIDE?

BY
GELETT BURGESS

Say! Ain't this book a 90-H. P., six-cylinder Seller? If WE do say it as shouldn't, WE consider that this man Burgess has got Henry James locked into the coal-bin, telephoning for " Information "

WE expect to sell 350 copies of this great, grand book. It has gush and go to it, it has that Certain Something which makes you want to crawl through thirty miles of dense tropical jungle and bite somebody in the neck. No hero no heroine, nothing like that for OURS, but when you've READ this masterpiece, you'll know what a BOOK is, and you'll sic it onto your mother-in-law, your dentist and the pale youth who dips hot-air into Little Marjorie until 4 Q. M. in the front parlour. This book has 42-carat THRILLS in it. It fairly BURBLES. Ask the man at the counter what HE thinks of it! He's seen Janice Meredith faded to a mauve magenta. He's seen BLURBS before, and he's dead wise. He'll say:

This Book is the Proud Purple Penultimate ! !

Burgess, who created a book jacket in 1907—featuring "Miss Melinda Blurb in the Act of Blurbing"—to mock a convention that was becoming more widespread in publishing.

Burgess coined the term, but credit for the thing itself should go to Walt Whitman. After reading the first edition of *Leaves of Grass* (1855), Ralph Waldo Emerson sent the poet a letter of praise. At the time, Emerson was a prominent intellectual, whereas Whitman was relatively unknown outside New York. The letter was meant to be a private word of encouragement. Whitman had it published in the *New York Tribune*. And one year later, in 1856, he had one line of the letter—"I greet you at the beginning of a great career"—stamped in gold leaf on the spine of the book's second edition. It's no surprise that the poet whose first great poem begins "I celebrate myself" had a flair for self-promotion.[3]

Indeed, Whitman knew that book covers are not only advertisements for the books themselves but also advertisements for the kinds of readers we imagine ourselves as being, or would like to be. There is an intimate connection between what we read and who we are, between shelves and selves. Finish reading a book, and its cover serves as a souvenir commemorating a transportive reading experience. Finish reading an *especially difficult* book, and its cover functions more like a trophy awarded for intellectual labor. Carry a book around in public, and its cover can betray you to other people who will make assumptions about you. It feels risky to be so exposed, but at times such assumptions are welcome, as when a book cover, flashed across a crowded subway car, operates like a secret handshake with another person reading the same.

The second edition of Walt Whitman's *Leaves of Grass*, published in 1856, with praise by Ralph Waldo Emerson printed in gold leaf on the spine. The philosopher, who wrote these words in a private letter to the poet, did not intend for them to be made public in this way.

A safeguard, a frame, a bridge, a translation, an interpretation, a teaser, a souvenir, a trophy, a handshake, and more—the book cover is many things. And it performs many functions. It is for this reason that we think of the book cover as a medium, whose multiple platforms (e.g., paper jacket, paperback, digital image) work together to represent the text visually and to present the book to the world. The term "medium" has several overlapping meanings, which allows it to capture the various identities and functions of the book cover in our time. Its cognates "mediation" and "mediator" suggest processes of intervention and brokering: unhappy couples pursue divorce mediation; middle-school students can see peer mediators instead of going to the principal's office. Since the sixteenth century, "medium" has been used to discuss the middle ground, quality, degree, or condition: the state of being in between two things. For instance, in *The Art of Distillation* (1651)—a distant precursor to today's home-brewing and mixology guides, with a dash of alchemy and medical science thrown in—John French describes one of his concoctions as "a saltish slime, and in taste, a Medium betwixt salt and Nitre." At the same time, "medium" also designated any intervening substance that can carry expressions, sensations, and moods; "the air," wrote one philosopher in 1643, "is the medium of musick and of all sounds." And alongside these meanings were two others: the idea of currency or the medium of exchange (e.g., any token of value used in a trading system) and the idea of the spiritual medium (e.g., a person claiming to be in contact with the dead).[4] This last meaning is not so far-fetched, since a main job of the book cover is to concretize the abstract, to visualize the ephemeral, and to render the metaphysical.

Later, in the nineteenth century, "medium" began to take on the more modern meanings that we know today. On the one hand, there is the idea of a communications medium: a channel of expression or an information delivery system through which signals flow back and forth. This idea intersects with our sense of "the media" as a vast system of journalism and entertainment that includes newspapers and magazines, television, talk radio, and the internet, as well as the many people who work as content producers, editors, influencers, and pundits. On the other hand, there is the idea of an artistic medium: painting, sculpture, dance, film, and so on. In the arts, the term refers to both *the material* and *the mode* of creation: clay or marble or papier-mâché can be considered the medium of sculpture, but sculpture, too, is a medium in its own right. And to speak of sculpture as a medium is not merely to discuss its materials, but to invoke an ancient and venerable aesthetic practice, whose meanings and values have been debated for millennia by artists, philosophers, and critics. This expansive notion of medium encompasses the histories, theories, and creative techniques of any art.[5]

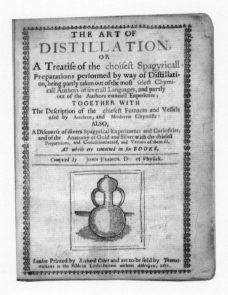

An early use of the term "medium" to refer to the space between two things, conditions, or qualities is found within *The Art of Distillation*, 1651.

So, what does it mean to think of the book cover as a medium? It is to see the book cover as a thing-between-things, a middle ground between text and context, a zone of interaction between the writer's vision and the culture in which the book is published. Further, it is to see the book cover as a *mediator* or *intermediary* that testifies to the social dimension of writing—for even if manuscripts are individually authored, books are collectively made, and their covers emerge through a process that involves many interested parties, not only the author and the designer, but also the editor, the publisher, the marketing director, the printer, and more.

Covers demand collaboration; the design process involves iteration, feedback, and revision. The end result is the production of an information-rich medium and, perhaps, also a work of art.

To be sure, most book covers are not works of art, but commodity packages. Nearly all book covers, however, are mixed-media productions that combine verbal and visual elements. Marshall McLuhan tells us that "the 'content' of any medium is always another medium," and this claim seems especially apt for the book cover, which recycles drawings, photographs, and text from book reviews and other sources.[6] Take, for instance, the cover of Yaa Gyasi's *Homegoing* (2016). Its original design was revised to include unexpected praise from Ta-Nehisi Coates—"*Homegoing* is an inspiration"—which Coates had issued via tweet. This is a perfect example of what McLuhan means, and it also shows us how the book cover, in the twenty-first century, exists both within and alongside the digital environment. Another example is Claudia Rankine's *Citizen* (2014), whose cover presents a photograph of a wall sculpture—David Hammons's *In the Hood* (1993)—that invokes the history of lynching. Here, an artwork is displayed via photography as part of an overall visual design.

McLuhan's claim draws our attention to remediation—the process whereby one medium cannibalizes another—which never ceases in a digital culture of endless sharing and remixing. The book cover plays a role in this process as both vehicle for and object in it. (This is one of the reasons, as we discuss in chapter four, why the book cover matters today.) A highly political work of art that addresses racism in America, *Citizen* itself was remediated in an apparent act of protest leading up to the 2016 US presidential election. Frustrated by the remarks of then candidate Donald Trump at a campaign rally in Illinois, a Black woman quietly opened her copy of *Citizen* and began to read, holding the book at eye level and exposing its cover directly to the television cameras. When reprimanded by an older white man, she refused to put the book down, and the video of their exchange went viral, remediated as an animated GIF.

Book covers within a wider media ecology. *Below:* A tweet that was remediated as a blurb. *Opposite:* An article of clothing that was remediated as a sculpture that was remediated as a photograph that was remediated as a book cover (*left; Citizen* by Claudia Rankine, designed by John Lucas) that was remediated as a prop (*right*).

> **Ta-Nehisi Coates** ✔
> @tanehisicoates
>
> [Follow] ⌄
>
> ## Yaa Gyasi's Homegoing is an inspiration
>
> 5:49 AM
>
> **782** Retweets **3,094** Likes
>
> 💬 15   ↻ 782   ♡ 3.1K   ✉

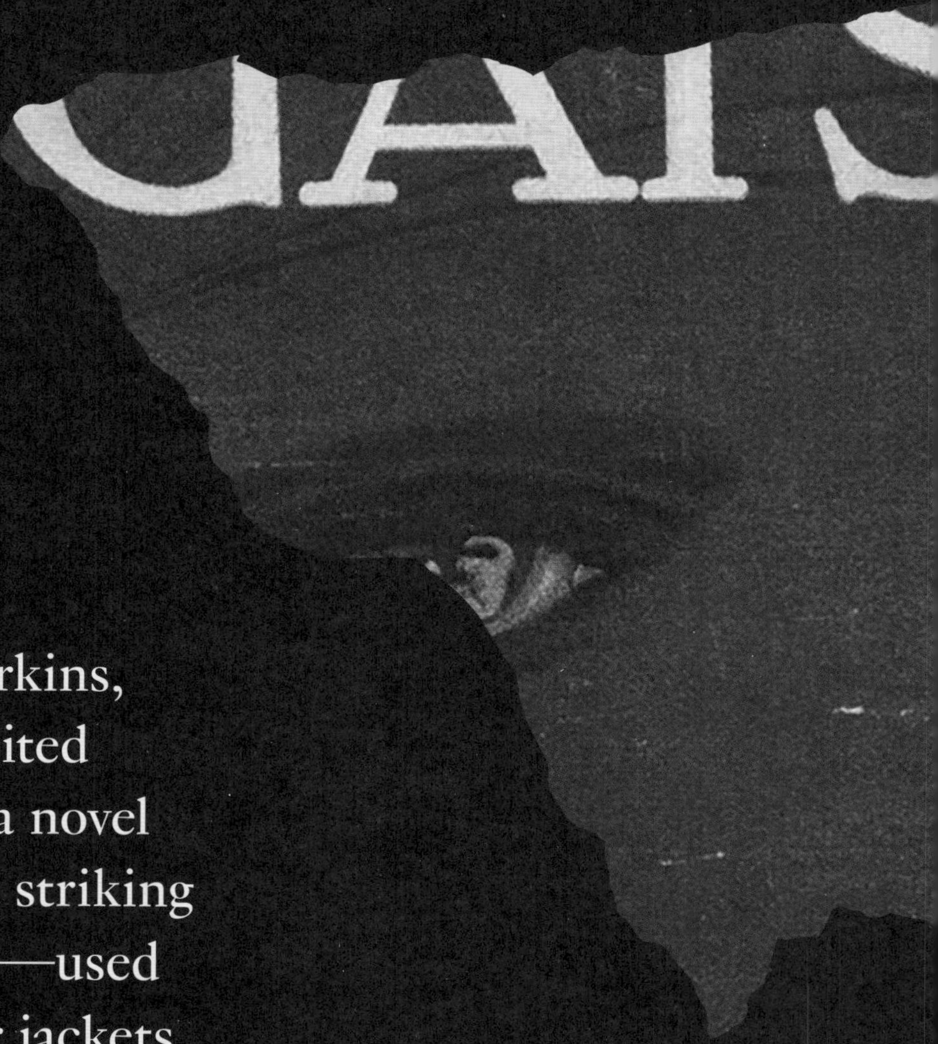

Even Maxwell Perkins,
the man who edited
The Great Gatsby—a novel
with one of the most striking
covers ever created—used
to discard the paper jackets
of his hardbacks.

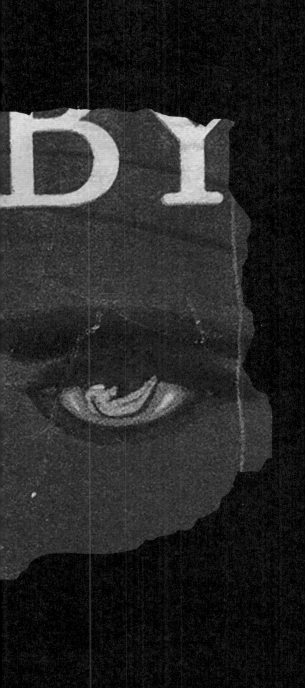

While it's easy to see the book cover as a medium of communication and information, embedded within an ecology of media that includes tweets and GIFS, it can be difficult to accept the book cover as a medium of art. As we discuss in chapter two, the twentieth century saw several phases of transformative cover design, and the work of the most influential cover designers is considered museum-worthy. But in general, book covers are treated as commercial schlock and ancillary ephemera, incidental rather than essential to literature or to any writing that appears in book form. Even Maxwell Perkins, the man who edited *The Great Gatsby* (1925)—a novel with one of the most striking covers ever created—used to discard the paper jackets of his hardbacks. (He also winced whenever he saw someone lick a finger before turning a page.)[7]

Ambivalence, it seems, surrounds the book cover. On the one hand, publishers spend considerable resources (time and money) on cover design; internet listicles rank the best designs of a given season; and cover designers get profiled in venues that run the gamut from airline in-flight magazines to the *New Yorker*. On the other hand, book covers are routinely trashed for sexism, racism, or pandering to the audience; their creators are hemmed in on all sides by the demands of the editor, the author, and the marketing department; and the Amazon interface requires the cover to look good as a tiny thumbnail.

Detail from the jacket for the first edition of *The Great Gatsby* by F. Scott Fitzgerald, designed by Francis Cugat.

What explains this ambivalence? One answer has to do with the shifting status of art—that is, with the question of whether art constitutes a special domain of existence, separate from the coarse concerns of life. According to the aesthetic philosophy of Immanuel Kant, who defined art as "purposiveness without purpose," aesthetic objects are autonomous: they serve no end and they exist in a realm apart.[8] Influential artists and critics championed this idea during the first half of the twentieth century, and this idea remains with us today. The book cover, however, not only serves a clear instrumental purpose but also depends on another medium, namely the manuscript text, so calling it art means challenging predominant ideas about what art is, even if we know that aesthetic autonomy is a fantasy and that art is so much more entangled with life than Kant argued.

But there is another reason for the ambivalence surrounding the book cover, which is that it can feel like a gimmick, even in cases of good design.

Gimmicks are little tricks intended to attract attention, publicity, or business. Cultural critic Sianne Ngai calls gimmicks "not-so-marvelous-marvels," and she notes that we tend to feel ambivalent about them.[9] Gimmicks appear everywhere in package design, and book covers can be ostentatiously gimmicky. They can be tricked out with production techniques—die cuts, spot glossing, foil stamps, coated paper stock—that are not only irritatingly captivating or captivatingly irritating but also unfriendly to the user, much like the deckled edge, which subtly reinforces the status of the literary classic while making it difficult to turn the pages. Such gimmicks are nothing new. In his influential discussion of "paratexts"—the material that surrounds the main text of a book—literary theorist Gérard Genette noted that book covers were becoming gimmickier. Books were being issued in boxes, the boxes were being covered in wrappers, and "posters, blow-ups of covers, and other gimmicks" were being created by publishers to lure fresh "clientele" into bookstores.[10]

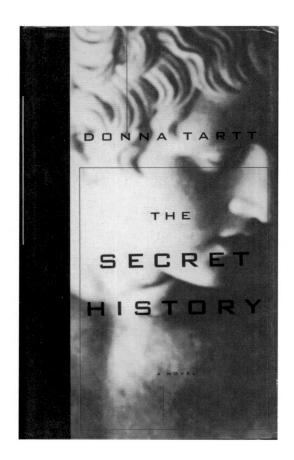

Opposite: Paul Sahre's die-cut and embossed jacket for *Watergate* by Thomas Mallon (*left*). Barbara de Wilde and Chip Kidd's acetate jacket for *The Secret History* by Donna Tartt (*right*). *Left:* Paul Sahre's word-less cover for *Killing the Buddha* by Peter Manseau and Jeff Sharlet. *Below:* Chip Kidd's three-cover book design for Vertical Press's *Ashes* by Kenzo Kitakata. *Bottom:* Jeff Middleton and Rodrigo Corral's glow-in-the-dark cover for *Haunted* by Chuck Palahniuk.

Production Techniques.

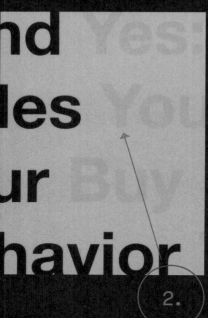
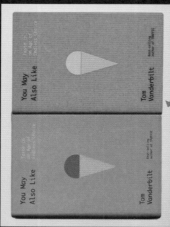

1. Die Cut
2. Blind Spot Gloss
3. One Book, Two Jackets
4. Blind Deboss
5. Foil Stamp
6. Metallic Ink

7. Perforation
8. Pre-printed Case
9. Pigment Stamp
10. Edge Staining
11. Traditional Deboss
12. Vellum Jacket
13. Moving Parts

Of course, book designers needn't rely on such tricks. They can create plain, text-based covers emphasizing the title and the author's name. Such design, known as the "big book look," works best for famous authors (Zadie Smith, Jonathan Franzen) whose names alone serve as marketing copy. But what about lavishly illustrated book jackets, or big-budget, high-concept productions that pull out all the stops to attract your attention? Are they always gimmicks? No, not always—not if they function as genuine interpretations of the text. Not if they provide, via imagery and texture, a reading of the text at hand, a reading that complements (or even challenges) your own sense of the text.

$3.00
net

**leave
cancelled**
by nicholas
monsarrat

They had twenty-four hours in which to be together. They were to have had more, but at the last moment his leave was cancelled. So they had but twenty-four hours in which to savor the full quality of their relationship—in which to talk, to laugh, to understand, and to forgive; in which to plan for days and nights that might never come; in which to love with all the passion of first fulfillment. For this brief span of time was a segment both of the honeymoon they had been denied and of the whole rich life together which they looked forward to and could only pray would not be denied them. From these few precious hours they must derive sustenance for the present and hope for the future.

Leave Cancelled is the full and honest recollection of every fleeting moment of that twenty-four hours, in the memories the man carried away with him, alive and warm and deeply cherished. It is a story that will be profoundly moving to all who know the poignancy of the too brief satisfaction of love, of life inexorably bounded by time.

Typography, binding, and jacket design by Paul Rand

Paul Rand's die-cut jacket for
Leave Cancelled by Nicholas Monsarrat,
Knopf, 1945.

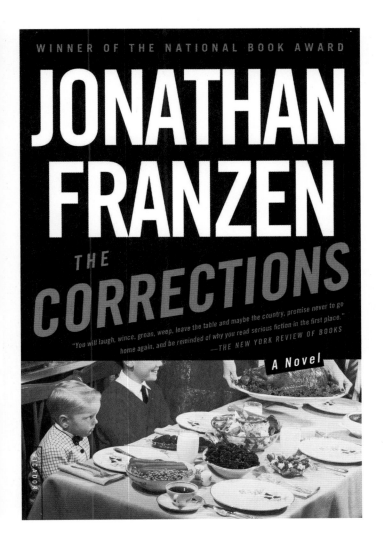

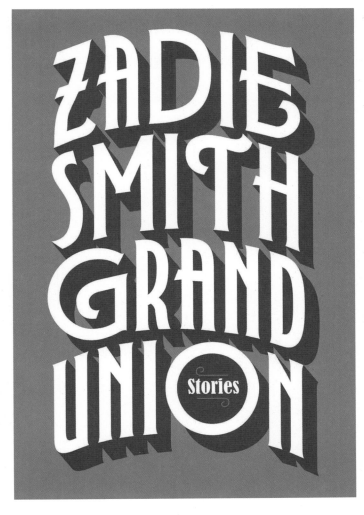

"In my experience, designing covers for 'big books' by 'big authors' is a similar process to designing any other book jacket—only more so. By which I mean: more people are involved, with more opinions and higher expectations. Adding to the pressure, everyone usually wants something that is different and 'fresh' (but not too different! No one wants to take a chance when so much is on the line). Usually we're asked for 'big type' and something that 'really pops.' In any case, it's still a book, and I love books. And a 'big author' is often a big author because their books are great. So that is a big plus. If things get painful, I usually try to go back to the book itself. And the roller-coaster ride of a 'big book' can be a kind of rush, I guess—usually in retrospect, though. As far as *The Corrections*, in particular, I came across the cover image on a postcard being sold in Union Square. I skipped back to my computer, came up with the design rather fast, and got an approval quickly, as I remember." —Lynn Buckley, cover designer of *The Corrections* by Jonathan Franzen

"Designing these covers is a joy. My brief is generally: This is the new book by Zadie Smith. The cover needs to convey, 'This is the new book by Zadie Smith.' Zadie is great at sharing her own ideas and thoughts for the cover but in a totally non-constrictive way. She will send things she likes, and I will be told the mood and setting and then left to get on with it. She is also very good at choosing titles. All of which balances perfectly. Detail and image are stripped away, and you try to give a sense of the content purely through text and color." —Jonathan Gray, cover designer of *Grand Union* by Zadie Smith

All-type jackets—for when the title and the author's name are enough.

Joan Didion The White Album

The most interesting book covers are those that, no matter how ornate, hold something back, requiring you to finish the text in order to "get" them. They feel less like tricks and more like wonders, revealed slowly through an interplay between the author's words and the designer's vision. They have a *timed-release* quality: they change with you as you read, and their meaning arrives later.

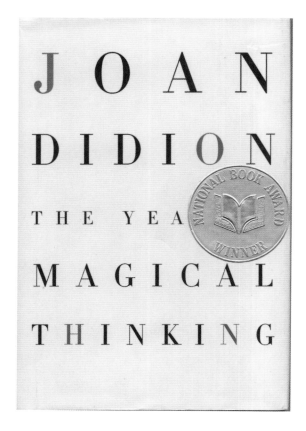

The word "John" (for John Gregory Dunne) emerging from Carol Devine Carson's jacket treatment for Joan Didion's memoir of loss, *The Year of Magical Thinking*.

"There may be something to magical thinking. As I began to design this jacket, still under the spell of Joan's manuscript, I began to arrange the lettering, and the name 'John' simply appeared to me. I hoped it would be a subtle way to honor him." —Carol Devine Carson

What emerges, say, out of the constellation of images on the cover of W. G. Sebald's *The Rings of Saturn*, designed by Peter Mendelsund?

THE RINGS OF SATURN

W.G. SEBALD

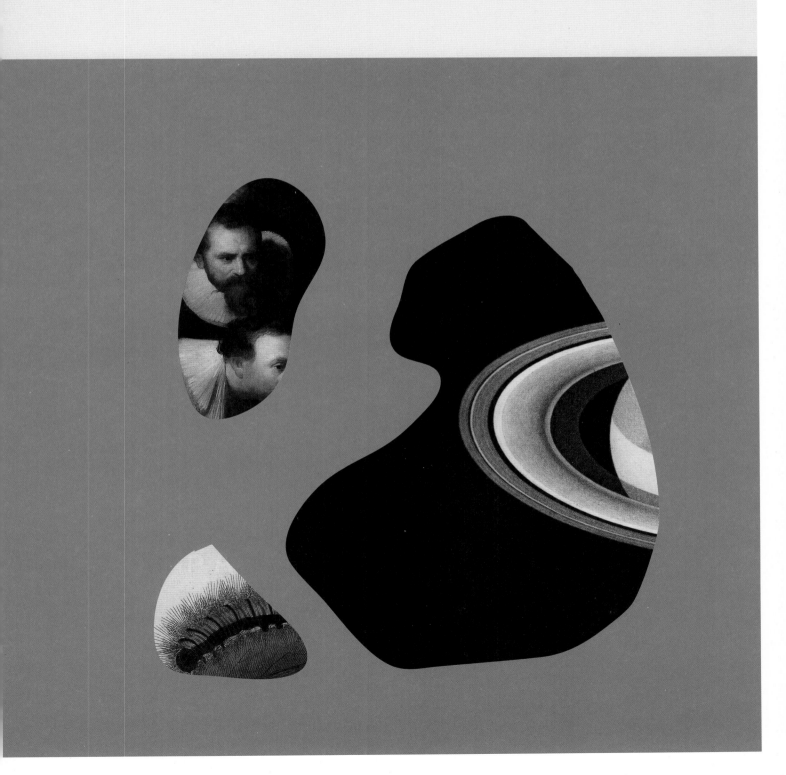

"The objective on the *Jurassic Park* cover was not so much to make it look like a 'big book' (though, of course, that would be a by-product) as it was to make it look like a book about dinosaurs that hopefully didn't look like any book about dinosaurs you had ever seen. Since we were kids, we had all enjoyed 'artists' conceptions' of what these animals might have looked like, but they inevitably came off as fake, because so much had to be built from the imagination. I decided to start with what was real, what we knew actually existed, and fill in just enough of the blanks to make it plausible yet unique. It didn't hurt (so to speak) that the result has so many sharp edges. In terms of the typography, the title is meant to evoke park signage. I will admit that, to this day, I can't remember why I put a black drop shadow behind his name. It looks needless and dumb. Who knows, maybe someone in sales said it needed to 'pop more.'" —Chip Kidd

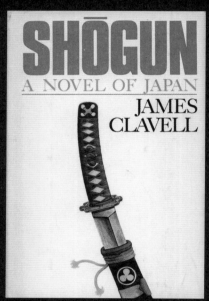

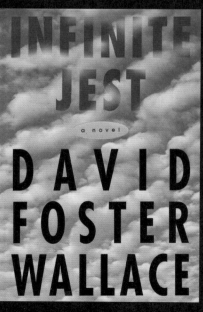

Clockwise from left: Jurassic Park by Michael Crichton, jacket design by Chip Kidd; Shōgun by James Clavell, jacket design by Paul Bacon; Infinite Jest by David Foster Wallace, jacket design by Steve Snider; Catch-22 by Joseph Heller, jacket design by Paul Bacon. Opposite: Coma by Robin Cook, jacket design by Paul Bacon.

The
Big Book
Look

1. Very Large Typography: The larger the better. Generally, there is one object of focus: the author's name or the title, though sometimes both. The type is often condensed to allow for the larger treatment.

2. Blurb: A common but not mandatory element.

3. Relatively Small, Emblematic Imagery: This is typically a single person, animal, or object.

4. Very Small Reading Line: This includes the "a novel (by)" line, movie tie-in information, etc.

5. Negative Space: Paul Bacon's jacket for Meyer Levin's *Compulsion* (see page 153) is widely thought to have inaugurated the tradition of employing negative space to offset the size of big-book typography.

6. Single Color Background: This allows text to stand out as figure against background.

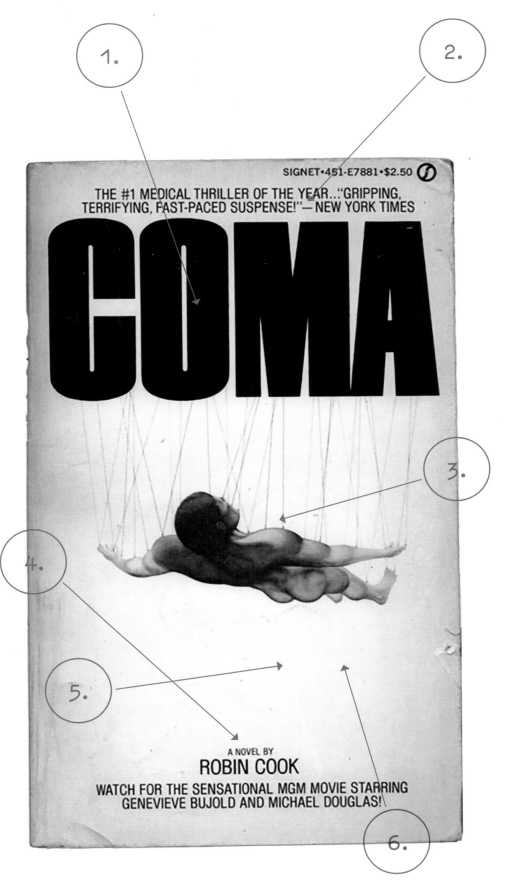

Take, for example, the original North American jacket for Tom McCarthy's novel *Satin Island* (2015). The narrator of *Satin Island* is a corporate anthropologist, tasked with writing the definitive ethnography of our time, or what the novel ironically calls The Great Report. His job is to sum up the hyperconnected condition of contemporary life, to explain how people live amid ubiquitous Wi-Fi and digital networks, which are layered, hierarchical, and controlled, perhaps by "some nefarious cabal."[11] Replicating the novel's motifs of layering and connection, the book jacket (see page 87) presents a grid, a rectilinear network of nodes and vertices, partially obscured by splotches of oil. An important historical figure in the novel is French anthropologist Claude Lévi-Strauss, who wrote that a "myth proposes a grid," and this book cover visualizes one of Lévi-Strauss's key ideas about how myths work in culture. Myths, he argued, make all the diverse elements of a culture seem like part of a single, coherent narrative, even as "scattered givens fail to link up and usually collide with one another."[12] The novel represents this theme through its narrator's struggle to finish The Great Report in a chaotic world, while the book cover juxtaposes the rational order of the grid with a ballistic splatter of ink, a myth exploded by an excess and spillage of meaning.

There's more to this cover. In addition to announcing title and author, the text makes a claim about the genre of the book at hand. *Satin Island* is A NOVEL, yes, but also A̶ T̶R̶E̶A̶T̶I̶S̶E̶, A̶N̶ E̶S̶S̶A̶Y̶, A̶ R̶E̶P̶O̶R̶T̶, A̶ M̶A̶N̶I̶F̶E̶S̶T̶O̶, and A̶ C̶O̶N̶F̶E̶S̶S̶I̶O̶N̶. The boundaries separating literary genres have become very porous in recent years. While some highbrow authors have turned to science fiction, fantasy, crime, and horror for inspiration, others, such as McCarthy, are trying to denude the novel of its fictionality— that is, to bring it as close to nonfiction as possible.[13] What happens, in such cases, is that the novel starts to resemble something else, some other genre of writing, although it never ceases being a novel, and the text on the cover illustrates this point. As a genre, the novel is both elastic and voracious: it can withstand tremendous variation as it ingests other genres—like the essay or the manifesto—in a way that simultaneously cancels and retains their rhetorical force. Just as we see ESSAY and MANIFESTO under erasure here, so too do we hear the muffled sounds of these genres in McCarthy's narration.

This cover, then, is not mere decoration, for it aims to play a deliberate role in our overall aesthetic experience of the book. Such experience amounts to more than just reading the text. A physical book is a mixed-media object that

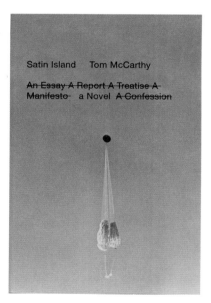

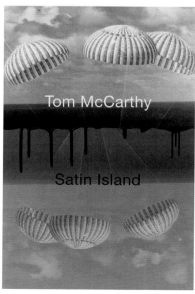

Unpublished cover explorations by Peter Mendelsund of Tom McCarthy's *Satin Island*. *Opposite:* The oleaginous. *This page:* Parachutes.

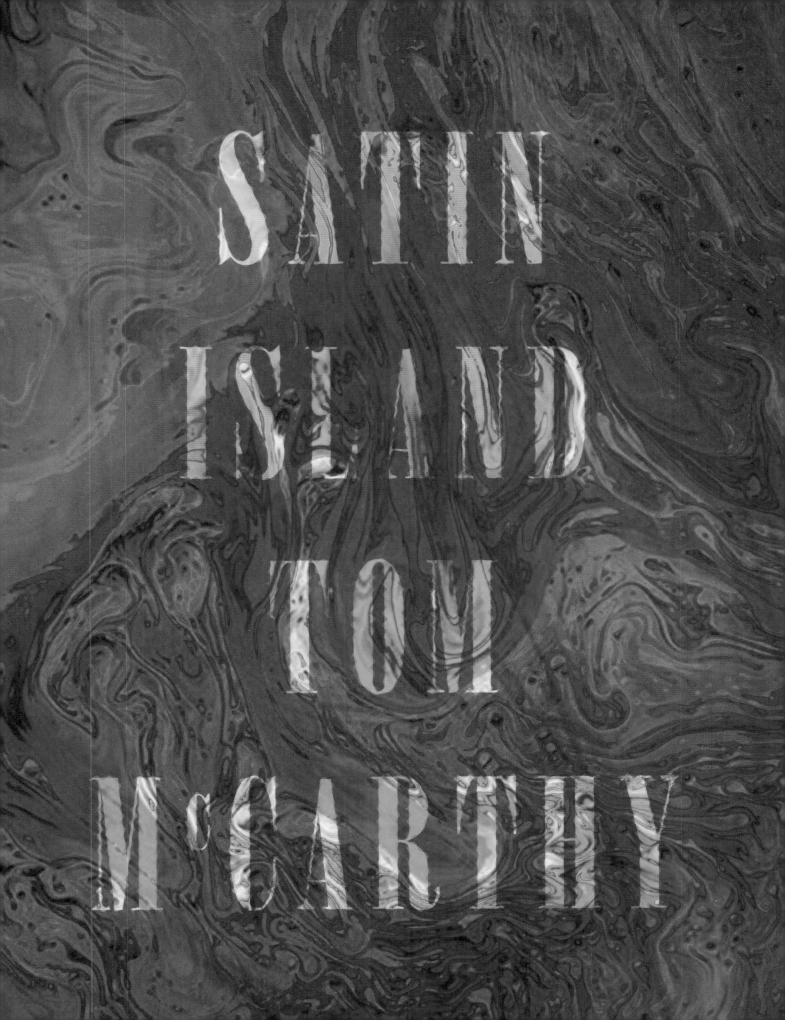

SATIN ISLAND

TOM McCARTHY

activates the eyes, hands, ears, and occasionally even the nose. Comics and graphic novels, for instance, make full use of the book as a visual object, which is why designing their covers can be especially tricky. Does the story begin on the cover? Is the cover designer, in this case, a sort of coauthor?

Literary authors, too, experiment with what might be called the phenomenology of the book in the digital age. Mark Z. Danielewski's debut novel *House of Leaves* (2000), for instance, provides a prime example of ergodic literature, which is literature that demands a "nontrivial effort" from the reader to traverse the text—an effort that goes beyond merely scanning black marks and turning pages.[14] The term "leaves," printed in blue ink throughout, resembles a hyperlink and anticipates the blue of the Facebook interface. More recently, Danielewski published *The Fifty-Year Sword*, which is more like an artist's book than a traditional novel.[15] Of its one thousand first-edition English copies, one is signed "Mark Danielewski," and fifty-one others are signed in marker with a "Z," which varies in color to coincide with the five colored quotation marks identifying different speakers in the text. With these choices, Danielewski simultaneously challenges conventional reading habits and extends the meaning of his work beyond the text to include the entire book and its various editions.

If all this seems gimmicky, however, it's because we're not accustomed to conflating literature with the book arts. We might acknowledge the differences among the periodical publication, the first edition, the hardcover, the paperback, the e-book, and the audiobook, but *Ulysses* is still *Ulysses* no matter what media format it takes. (Another way to make this point is to say that you can't forge a novel as you can forge a painting: any exact copy of *Ulysses*, rewritten by someone other than James Joyce, is the real thing.) And yet, literature has been the occasion for some of the most incredible book art ever produced, and *Ulysses* in particular has stimulated a rich history of cover design since its initial publication in the United States in 1934. In the next chapter, a look at this history will help to clarify what distinguishes the book cover in our time.

Interior page
of *House of
Leaves* by Mark
Z. Danielewski,
designed by
the author.

*Opposite: Satin
Island* by Tom
McCarthy, jacket
design by Peter
Mendelsund.

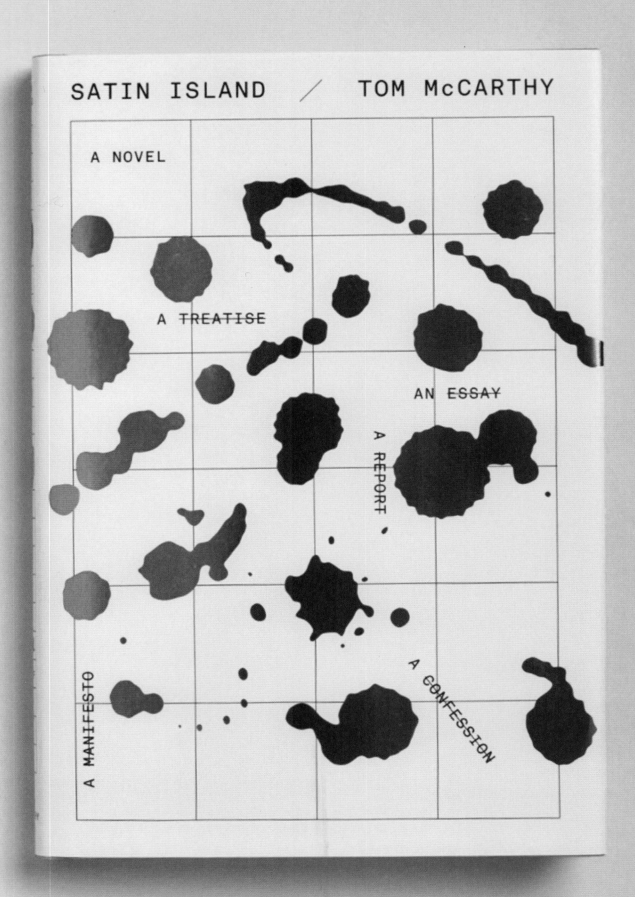

"Book covers protect books, but they also
identify them by delimiting their content.
Because the pages are secured between
covers, we feel confident that we know just
what belongs to any one book. We have a
means of marking the distinction between
its inside and its outside. Paradoxically,
however, there's a long tradition of covering
books with pieces from other books—thereby
creating 'Frankenstein books,' as librarians
sometimes put it. In printing houses before
the nineteenth century, printer's waste—the
name for the paper scraps that under more
auspicious circumstances would have ended
up being pages in books themselves—wasn't
always discarded, but instead was quite often
pressed into use either to form the protective
wrapper placed around a book or to stiffen
a book's spine or its boards. After the
dispersal of the monastic libraries during
the English Reformation, Catholic manuscripts
were sometimes repurposed to just this effect,
indicating how they were at this point deemed
valuable only for their matter rather than
for their content. Book historians enjoy
tracking the incongruous juxtapositions this
sixteenth-century practice of recycling and
reuse, and of slicing and dicing, can create:
it's pretty fun, for instance, to discover the
bit of Catholic prayer book that is sheathing
the collection of Protestant sermons. The
motives that drove such practices were
sentimental as well pragmatic. In 1822, the
English essayist Charles Lamb wrote, for
instance, about his exasperation at seeing
texts he held in contempt—'these things in
books' clothing'—decked out in elaborate
bindings: as he imagined the shivering of
his own, beloved but worn-out books, Lamb
declared himself ready to 'strip' the hateful
imposters, so as 'to warm my ragged veterans in
their spoils.' Later in the nineteenth century,
Lamb's proposed program for re-clothing good
books using the outsides of mediocre ones was
adopted, furtively, by some sectors of the
antiquarian book trade. The term 'remboîtage'
came into use by the early twentieth century
to designate this rather deceptive practice
developed for the bibliophile market: reusing
old covers, which had been crafted and
decorated in famous workshops admired by
connoisseurs, by surreptitiously transferring
them to volumes deemed worthier than the ones
they had adorned originally."

—Deidre Lynch, book historian

2.

What the Book Cover Was

Book Covers through the Decades

1820s–1830s: Publishers begin wrapping books in undecorated paper coverings to protect illustrated boards. The first dust jackets appear.

1840s–1860s: Publishers begin replacing leather with fabric as their preferred book-binding material. Embossed or gold illustrations on fabric become more common. There are limited examples of illustrated jackets during this period.

1890s–1920: A significant increase in experimentation with jacket design is seen during this period. Initially, jackets replicate designs found on illustrated boards. Eventually, jackets exhibit original designs. Publishers add text to jacket flaps. The first "blurbs" appear. Boards become plainer as illustration moves to jackets.

1907: Gelett Burgess coins the term "blurb."

1920s: A major period of jacket design that coincides with the rise of Transatlantic Modernism and the emergence of graphic design as a distinct profession. Aaron Douglas designs covers for authors associated with Harlem Renaissance.

1922: W. A. Dwiggins coins the term "graphic designer."

1925: Book collectors begin preserving jackets. *The Great Gatsby* is published, with a cover by Francis Cugat.

1930s: The paperback era begins.

1931: W. A. Dwiggins designs H. G. Wells's *The Time Machine*.

1934: Ernst Reichl designs *Ulysses*.

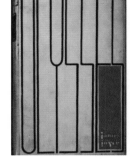

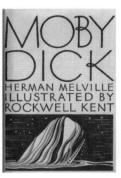

1915: Alfred A. Knopf publishes its first book with a striking orange cover.

1844: *The Vision; or Hell, Purgatory & Paradise of Dante Alighieri*, translated by Rev. Henry Francis Cary, MA.

1855: *Corsica and Napoleon*, translated from the German of Ferdinand Gregorovius, by Edward Joy Morris.

1883: George Lowell Austin, *Henry Wadsworth Longfellow: His Life, His Works, His Friendships*, illustrated.

1883: Louisa May Alcott, *Hospital Sketches and Camp and Fireside Stories*, with illustrations.

1894: The first issue of *The Yellow Book* is published. Its first art editor, Aubrey Beardsley, is credited with the idea for the yellow cover, which was associated with illicit French fiction of the period.

1930: Rockwell Kent illustrates *Moby-Dick*

1929: John T. Witerich asks, "How old is the dust-jacket?" in a column for *Publisher's Weekly*.

1935: Allen Lane launches Penguin Books. Edward Preston Young, age twenty-one, creates the now-iconic cover design.

1829: The Bodleian Library holds what is often cited as the first known book jacket: the paper wrapper for a gift book, bound in silk, entitled *Friendship's Offering*. There may be earlier examples. It is difficult to determine when, exactly, paper wrappers first emerged, since they were intended to be discarded.

1936: James Laughlin founds New Directions.

1940: Modern Library publishes James Joyce's *Ulysses*, which says "Complete and Unexpurgated" on its cover.

1940s: Book jackets are displayed in museums. Progressive designers push boundaries. The paperback revolution offers new platforms for cover design.

1947: Robert Jonas designs the cover for Henry James's *Daisy Miller* (Penguin).

1948: The Book Jacket Designers Guild holds the first exhibition of book jackets.

1949: An international book-jacket exhibition is unveiled at Victoria and Albert Museum, London.

1950s: Modernism persists through the middle of the twentieth century. The first "how-to" manual for cover designers is published. The "big book look" becomes conventional.

1953: Jason Epstein launches Anchor Books, and the "quality paperback" is born.

1953: James Avati, known as the "Rembrandt of Paperbacks," designs *The Catcher in the Rye*.

1955: *Lolita* published in Paris by Olympia Press, unadorned.

1956: Peter Curl publishes *Designing a Book Jacket*.

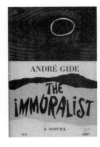

1939: Robert de Graff Launches Pocket Books in New York.

1941: Alvin Lustig designs the cover for Henry Miller's *The Wisdom of the Heart* (New Directions).

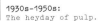

1930s–1950s: The heyday of pulp.

1954: Knopf founds Vintage Books, another quality paperback line.

1949: Charles Rosner publishes *The Art of the Book-Jacket*.

1949: E. McKnight Kauffer designs the cover for *Ulysses* (Random House).

1949: W. A. Dwiggins designs the cover for Willa Cather's *On Writing*.

1950s: *Compulsion* and the rise of the "big book look."

1960s–1970s: The commercial (and social realist) cover designs of Leonard Baskin and Antonio Frasconi are published.

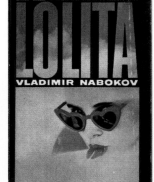

1980s: Postmodernism emerges in cover design. The "big book look" is resuscitated in the 1980s–1990s.

1962: Cover of *Lolita* with movie tie-in.

19568–1979: David Pelham, one of the most talented designers of his generation, produces memorable covers for Penguin Books.

1969: Paul Bacon designs the cover for *Portnoy's Complaint*.

1984: Vintage Contemporaries is launched with Postmodernist covers by Lorraine Louie and others.

1950s–1960s: Roy Kuhlman and other designers bring abstraction and surrealism to a larger market.

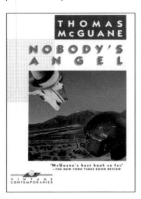

1965: The US Copyright office begins keeping a file on jackets containing biographical information and author photos.

1960: Pelican Books publishes the abstract, formatted cover for paperback nonfiction *The Divided Self*.

1986: Carin Goldberg designs the cover for *Ulysses*.

1960s–1970s: The "big book look" prevails. Modernism remains important, even as some designers look for alternatives. Paperbacks continue to flourish. Novels are adapted for cinema, and book covers mimic movie posters.

1961: Paul Bacon designs the cover for *Catch-22* (Simon & Schuster).

1960s–1970s: Psychedelia and the counterculture emerge onto book jackets.

1990s: The Knopf Years, photography is prevalent on covers for trade fiction and production effects flourish.

1980s: Photography supplants illustration as the primary medium for making covers for fiction.

2000s: The return of the illustration; the return of the coverless case; the death of Quark and the rise of Adobe software; handwriting returns, as does handcraft; parchment and other old papers are digitized and used as backgrounds for retro effects. Resuscitation of minimalism.

2010s: Internet culture and the rise of social media provide the conditions for the emergence of the cover-as-thumbnail.

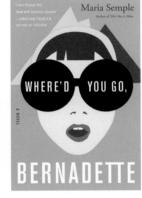

2012: Vector illustration hits the big time.

1989: Zone Books provides design-forward covers for academic titles.

1994: Amazon.com is founded

1995: The design of non-design becomes a trend.

2005: *On Bullshit*, and the rise of the little, minimally designed nonfiction title.

2007 & 2010: Amazon launches the Kindle, Apple follows with iBooks, and Ebook (only) covers emerge.

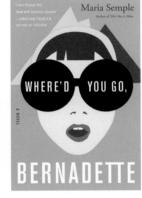

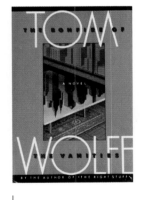

2010: The return of decorative covers, cloth cases, and pattern stamping.

2005: Ned Drew and Paul Sternberger publish *By Its Cover*; John Updike publishes "Deceptively Conceptual" in the *New Yorker*.

2018: The return of all-type, pre-formatted editions.

1980s–1990s: Fred Marcellino's 1987 jacket for *The Bonfire of the Vanities* and the ahead-of-their-time media juxtapositions of Andrzej Klimowski and Lawrence Ratzkin straddle the 80s and 90s.

2002: Jonathan Gray and others bring back the handwriting-driven (or, generally speaking, craft-driven) cover.

2010: The rise of the book cover tote.

2015: The beginning of the era of the interchangeable, big-type, colorful cover, a trend which could be thought of as the "it will work well as a thumbnail on Amazon" cover. Arguably, the end of the cover as interpretation or criticism.

In an unsigned review of James Fenimore Cooper's novel *The Red Rover*, republished by Putnam in 1850, Herman Melville argued that books "should be appropriately appareled."

The 1827 edition of James Fenimore Cooper's
The Red Rover seems to fulfill Herman Melville's
wishes for the look of the book.

Criticizing the "sad lack of invention" among bookbinders of his day, Melville longed for a more ambitious cover design than Putnam had offered. He suggested that an adventure novel about a pirate, the eponymous Red Rover, should not have been covered so blandly; it deserved, instead, to be decked out in "a flaming suit of flame-colored morocco, as evanescently thin and gauze-like as possible, so that the binding might happily correspond with the sanguinary fugitive title of the book."[16] Apparently, Melville had not seen the 1827 edition. When *The Red Rover* was first published by Henry Colburn in London, Cooper's eighth novel was housed in a custom cloth chemise and a handsome red slipcase. The small octavos were bound in three-quarter calf gilt, with raised bands, brown calf spine labels, and marbled boards. To acquire this edition of *The Red Rover* today, rare book collectors would expect to spend more than $1,500.

This page: Alfred A. Knopf's first publication, Emile Augier's *Four Plays*, appeared in 1915 with a striking orange and blue cover.
In front: Mars in the House of Death by Rex Ingram, cover by W. A. Dwiggins, who coined the term "graphic designer."

The history of today's book covers stretches back to the time of Melville.[17] And this history still matters to twenty-first century book design, despite the changes that have occurred since the start of the digital revolution. Beginning in the 1820s, publishers began creating detachable paper coverings for their books. Prior to this, various other materials were used. A protective jacket made of human skin, with patches of hair removed to provide space for lettering, was created in 1310 and currently sits somewhere in the British Library.[18] The practice of binding books in human skin was not terribly uncommon, even in Melville's time. In 2014 Harvard University's Houghton Library confirmed that a book in its collection, Arsène Houssaye's *Des destinées de l'ame* (*On the Destiny of the Soul*), published in the mid-1880s, had been bound this way, using a technique known as anthropodermic bibliopegy.[19] When the book was donated to the library in 1934, it came with a note explaining that "a book about the human soul deserved to have a human covering."

Paper coverings, most commonly called dust jackets or dust wrappers, were used to protect the bindings from both scuffing and sunlight, and initially they were not illustrated. It wasn't until the 1890s that publishers began regularly employing the jacket as an advertising device, but even in this era, jackets tended to replicate imagery from either the decorated bindings or the inside of the book. Lavishly illustrated jackets, surrounding unadorned hardbacks, did not become prevalent until the 1920s. Some of the first modern book covers were designed in the Soviet Union by Russian Constructivists Alexander Rodchenko and El Lissitzky. During this time in both the United States and England, publishers began to hire book designers, to assemble art departments, and to invest more heavily in graphic design and promotion. The advertising industry had taken off, and books needed to sell themselves in a competitive marketplace.

When Alfred A. Knopf founded his imprint in 1915, for instance, he issued his first book, *Four Plays* by Emile Augier, in striking orange and blue. By the 1920s, Knopf had earned a reputation for its investment in the aesthetics of physical books; over the past century, many prominent designers have done work for Knopf. Indeed, the very designer who coined the term "graphic designer," W. A. Dwiggins, began working on Knopf books in the 1920s, around the same time that Willa Cather signed with the imprint, convinced that Knopf "had set out to do something unusual and individual in publishing."[20] (Not that Cather was always easy to please: "Miss Cather was absolutely horrified at the sight of the title page for *Death Comes for the Archbishop*," Knopf wrote to book designer Elmer Adler on April 27, 1927, "and I am afraid I could not be very enthusiastic about it."[21])

As in other fields of art and design, the decades between World War I and World War II were especially fertile. Modernism had swept across Europe, and many of the most influential jacket designers through the 1930s were immigrants to the United States, who had brought with them the aesthetic sensibilities of Futurism, Constructivism, and the Bauhaus. The work of Ladislav Sutnar, György Kepes, Rockwell Kent, George Salter, Ernst Reichl, and E. McKnight Kauffer stands out from this time. In the UK, Vanessa Bell, a member of the

Arsène Houssaye's *Des destinées de l'ame,* published in
the mid-1880s and bound in human skin.

Bloomsbury Group, produced striking jackets for books by her sister Virginia Woolf. Notable work was also happening on the continent. In France the look of the book was standardized—yellow paper jackets with black letterpress type prevailed—but Germany during the Weimar Republic was a site of avant-garde experimentation, whose varied techniques included photomontage, pictorial typography, and painting. Of course, vibrant book cultures existed elsewhere in the world, but jacket design as we know it today sprouted from Transatlantic Modernism.

This is one reason why the quintessential Modernist novel, James Joyce's *Ulysses*, has such a rich history of coverings and re-coverings, beginning with its initial 1922 publication in book form by Sylvia Beach, who was instructed by Joyce to wrap the book in blue to match the Aegean Sea. (Now that this edition has aged for nearly a hundred years, though, it appears more green than blue, more Irish than Greek.) First published as a book in Paris, *Ulysses* was deemed obscene and thus unpublishable in the United States, until a US District Court decided otherwise in 1933.[22]

The cover of its first US edition is no less iconic than the original. Set in Futura Black, a typeface designed by Paul Renner in 1927, the text on Ernst Reichl's 1934 cover for Random House dominates the front flap. When Reichl got the *Ulysses* job, he was a thirty-three-year-old, German-born designer with a PhD in art history and literature, who had come to New York in 1926. Unlike many of his peers, he was a "whole book designer," not only a cover artist, and believed that careful reading of the manuscript was the basis for good design. Exploiting the figurative power of letters, perhaps in a nod to Joyce's love of acrostics, Reichl created a cover image that depicts the elongated wandering of Leopold Bloom, the novel's protagonist, through the city of Dublin. The ostentatious verticality of the image is offset by subtle horizontal lines at the top, bottom, and middle, and the black text is counterbalanced by a single bold rectangle on the bottom right corner, suggesting, perhaps, Bloom's occasional audacity as a thinker and social actor.

A first edition of James Joyce's *Ulysses*, published in Paris by Sylvia Beach's Shakespeare and Company in 1922. The book is a paperback whose colors (white lettering against a blue background) were suggested by Joyce himself to match those of the Greek flag.

ULYSSES

BY

JAMES JOYCE

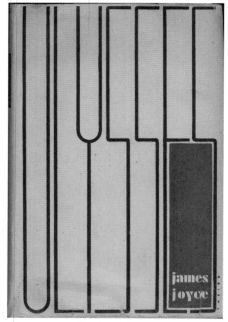

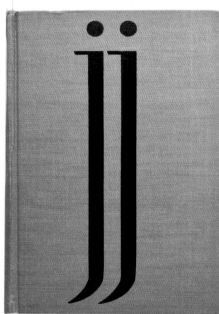

Ulysses, Reichl said, is "the best known design I ever made," although the "influence of Mondrian" is purely "imagined." Like any good designer, Reichl could be critical of the details: since the jacket was "designed for a 6 × 9 book, the 5½ x 8 volume is a bit cramped." But he tolerated subsequent re-coverings of the novel in his lifetime. "The book is now a classic," he wrote. "Classics generally do not remain in their original format. *Ulysses*, in this respect at least, is no exception."[23] Fifteen years later, also working for Random House, E. McKnight Kauffer likewise employed text as a compositional device on his cover for the novel. The exaggerated "U" and "L" refer back to Reichl's pioneering design, while the stark black background calls to mind the mid-century abstraction of Ad Reinhardt, rather than the earlier work of Piet Mondrian.

In 1986 Carin Goldberg created the cover for the so-called corrected edition of *Ulysses*, and she used Futura, too, in a design that takes Renner's 1928 *Applied Arts of Bavaria* poster as a template. Goldberg's cover was criticized for its overreliance on pastiche, but it remains a touchstone of Postmodernist design. In 2002 Random House issued *Ulysses* in a facsimile of Reichl's 1934 jacket, uncredited and rendered digitally. This jacket provides an example of how twenty-first-century design also treats the history of Modernism as so much material to be quoted, as long as the details look good on a tablet or smartphone, not to mention in a selfie or shelfie.

How might *Ulysses* appear, how might it look and feel, all decked out for its centennial? On February 2, 2022, what combination of commercial, technological, and imaginative forces will bring about the 100th-anniversary book design that we all know is coming?

One way to answer this question is to look back at major movements and styles of cover design over the last hundred years, because today's cover designers have this history at their fingertips. Some cover designers have designated image researchers; everyone has Google. In the previous chapter, we suggested that the book cover should

Ulysses covers through the ages. *Top left:* The cover of the first US edition (1934), designed by Ernst Reichl using a typeface designed by Paul Renner. *Bottom left:* The case wrap of same. *Top right:* E. McKnight Kauffer's cover for the 1949 publication. *Bottom right:* Carin Goldberg's cover for the 1986 publication.

be considered a medium, and media theorist Friedrich Kittler tells us that "media determine our situation," meaning that technologies shape human experience.[24] But the opposite is also true: our situation determines media. There is a dialectical relationship between media and history that plays out in the case of book covers as a drama of repetitious repackaging: an iterative process of recasting literature as a visual and tangible thing. In other words, every historical period gets the *Ulysses* it deserves. Just as Joyce's words can take on different meanings depending on their context, so too the look of the book can say a lot about the moment in which it was produced.

Today's cover designers enjoy easy access to the visual cultures of the past. But they also face the challenge of creating good design for a discerning public, since increased screen time has made us all very sophisticated viewers. It's a challenge that their predecessors faced in their own ways, which explains why the history of the book cover includes such a wide variety of styles. Modernism, however, remained important through the middle of the twentieth century—and beyond, as the 2002 facsimile of Reichl's *Ulysses* suggests. Alvin Lustig, Elaine Lustig Cohen, Roy Kuhlman, and Paul Rand were among the most important mid-century Modernists, extending the tradition into the decades following World War II. As Modernists, these designers believed in the close relationship between theory and practice, and they tried to make covers that would fuse type and illustration into aesthetic wholes, as both Reichl and Kauffer had done. They also had strong civic ideals: "The designer," argued Alvin Lustig, "is not a single-minded specialist, but an integrator of all the art forms—and simultaneously a spokesman for social progress."[25] And they were employed by progressive publishers such as New Directions, Knopf, Doubleday, Viking, Penguin, and Grove. While the Lustigs sought to break down what they perceived to be the false boundary between "applied" and "fine" art, Rand worked to translate the visual language of the European avant-gardes for the American audience.

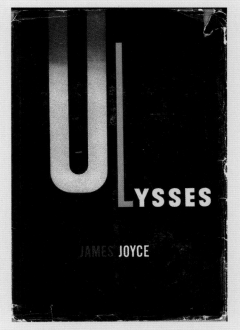

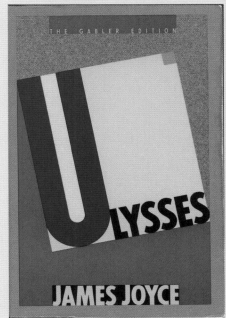

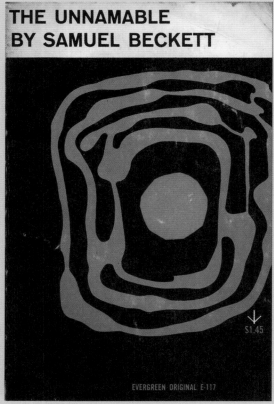

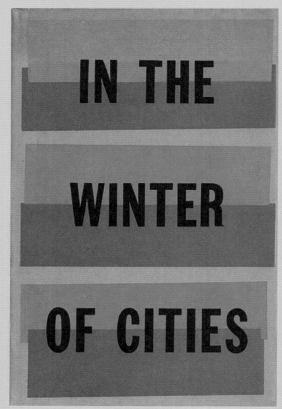

Mid-Century Modernisms. *Clockwise from left: Zen and Japanese Culture* by D. T. Suzuki, cover by Paul Rand; *The Unnamable* by Samuel Beckett, cover by Roy Kuhlman; *In the Winter of Cities* by Tennessee Williams, cover by Elaine Lustig Cohen. *Opposite: The Man Who Died* by D. H. Lawrence, jacket by Alvin Lustig.

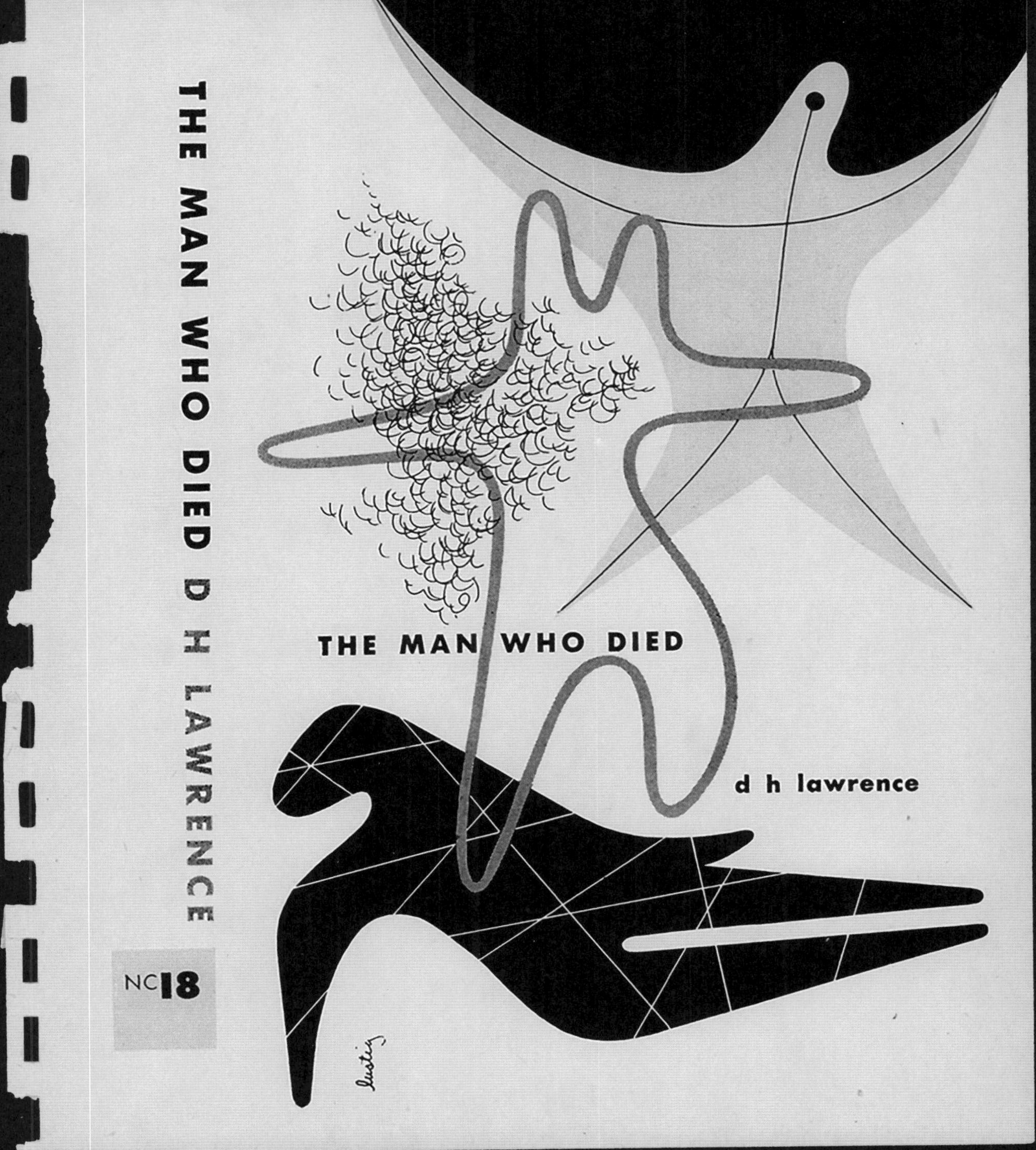

THE MAN WHO DIED D H LAWRENCE

NC**18**

THE MAN WHO DIED

d h lawrence

Meanwhile, in the UK, Art Deco prevailed through the 1940s, and its dynamic and geometric motifs appeared on notable jackets by Kent, Kauffer, Edmund Dulac, and an illustrator known only as Baird. After World War II, Britain saw the rise of Neoromanticism in the arts, a movement characterized by its elegiac mood and spiritual yearning for connection with the landscape. Inspired by the visionary paintings of Samuel Palmer and William Blake, Neoromantics such as Keith Vaughan, John Minton, Robert Medley, Edward Bawden, Edward Burra, and Michael Ayrton worked across the fine and applied arts. Their book covers, many of which were created for publisher John Lehmann, typically depict landscapes and vistas, overlaid with hand-rendered lettering in a relaxed style. At the same time, on both sides of the Atlantic, cover designers were turning their attention to children's books, and the work of Leo Lionni and Ferelith Eccles Williams is especially notable here.

By the mid-twentieth century, book-cover design had assumed an important place in the history of graphic art and communication, and like other arts during this period it showed both Realist and Modernist tendencies. Some covers, such as those by Ben Shahn, featured illustrations depicting characters, settings, or scenes from the text; others appeared, in the Modernist tradition, more abstract and formally austere. Following in the wake of Alvin Lustig and Rand, designers such as George Giusti, Fred Troller, Rudy de Harak, Anita Walker Scott, and the team of Chermayeff and Geismar pushed Modernism forward, while Milton Glaser and Seymour Chwast, both at Push Pin Studios, began developing a new eclectic style that fused illustration with historical typefaces.

The years between 1945 and 1970 were especially vibrant for book-cover design. The pioneering Modernists were still active, and the paperback book had emerged as an important platform for cover designers. Today, when a hardcover is republished as a paperback, it's usually issued with a different cover. There are several reasons why this might be so. It could be that the paperback publisher didn't acquire the rights to the earlier design, or that lower-than-expected hardcover sales prompted a redesign, or that the author and/or editor pushed

for a change. Many paperback publishers, moreover, have a distinctive identity that they want to remain consistent across all their products, so a new cover design will be needed to make the book conform to the aesthetic of the brand. There are also basic differences in size and price: the standard paperback is smaller and less expensive than the standard hardcover, so the paperback cover designer confronts a different set of constraints and possibilities.

Although the lavishly designed hardcover has attained the status of a luxury object, there's no denying the importance of the paperback to the history of cover art. Allen Lane founded Penguin Books, the first successful mass-market paperback line, in 1935. He was followed shortly thereafter in the United States by Robert de Graff, who launched Pocket Books in 1939. Their success paved the way for Avon, Popular Library, Dell, Bantam, and other imprints, including New American Library, publisher of both Signet (fiction) and Mentor (nonfiction). While book jackets are a nineteenth-century invention, paper bookbindings are nearly as old as print. In France, books have been bound in paper for centuries; the 1922 edition of *Ulysses*, for instance, is a paperback. In the United States, however, large-scale paperback publishing was attempted at least twice in the nineteenth century with only modest success.

Lane and de Graff were more successful, because they developed a new method of distribution and sales.[26] In the 1940s, '50s, and '60s, paperbacks were distributed with pulp magazines and comic books, meaning they were sold at newsstands, drugstores, smoke shops, lunch counters, and train and bus stations. Their covers had to be enticing enough to compete with any other retail object. Some designers, such as Robert Jonas, adapted high-Modernist aesthetics for the paperback. A friend of both Willem de Kooning and Arshile Gorky, Jonas has been credited with bringing Modernism to main street.[27] Take, for example, his design for Truman Capote's debut novel, *Other Voices, Other Rooms* (1948). With its image of a shattered windowpane framing an Edenic couple, the cover adapts a motif from Édouard Manet's *Le déjeuner sur l'herbe* (1863). Similarly, his cover for the 1947 Penguin paperback of Henry James's *Daisy Miller* adapts the stylistic features of Cubist collage.

Mechanical for Penguin Books, 1948, by Jan Tschichold and Erik Ellegaard Frederiksen, based on the original 1935 design by Edward Preston Young.

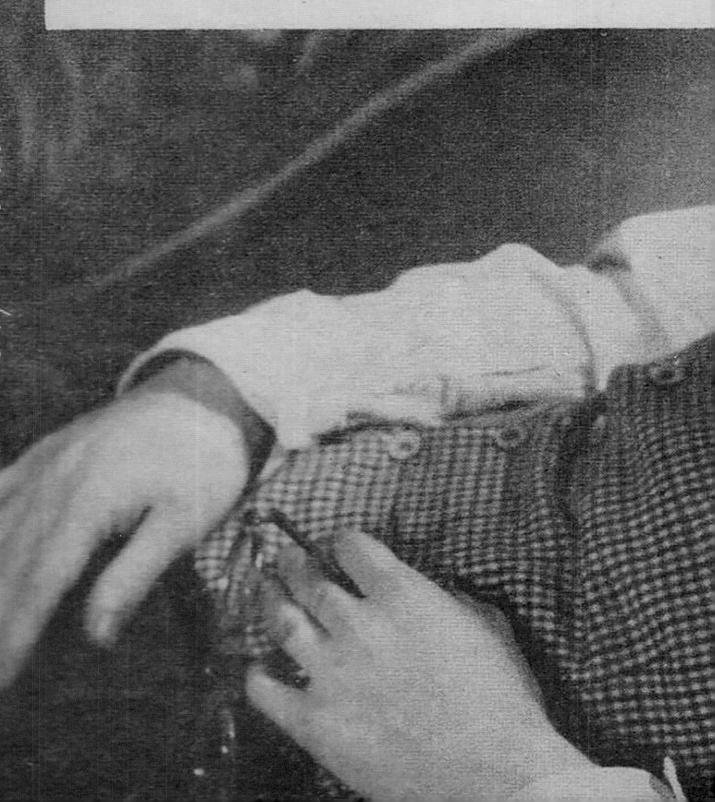

"**Rarely does one find a writer of Tru**
eration who shows, at the beginning o
results which would seem to come onl

Capote's gen-
s career, those
ith maturity."
RGUERITE YOUNG

Halma

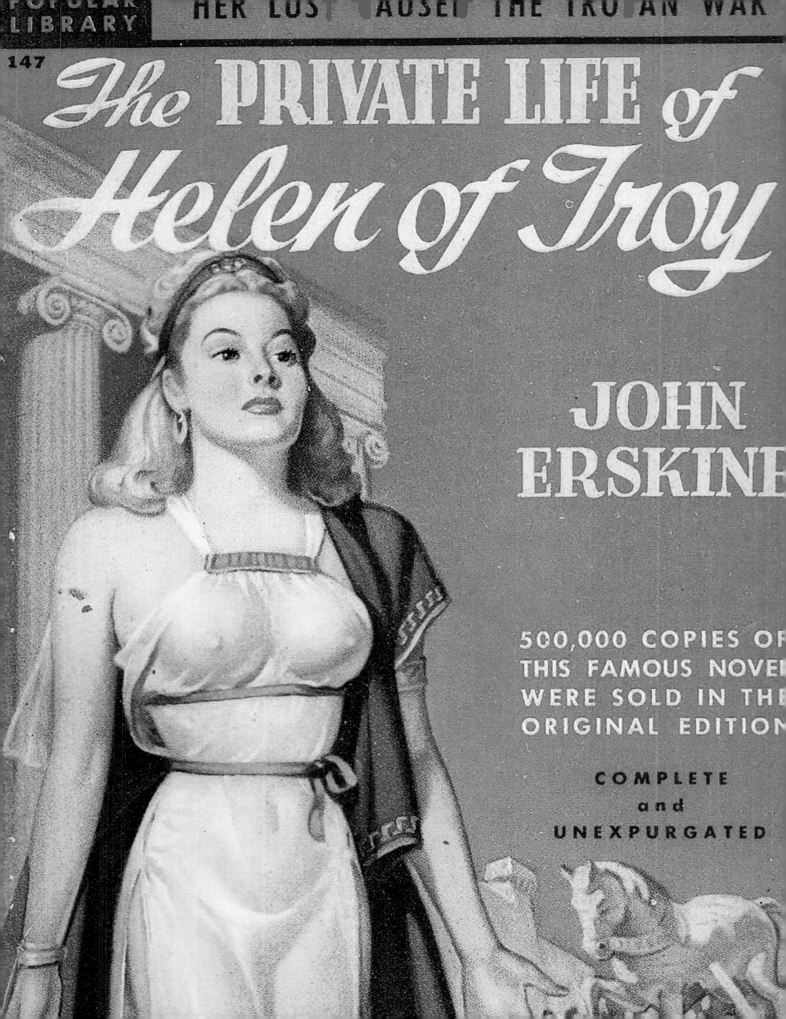

The PRIVATE LIFE of
Helen of Troy

JOHN ERSKINE

500,000 COPIES OF
THIS FAMOUS NOVEL
WERE SOLD IN THE
ORIGINAL EDITION

COMPLETE
and
UNEXPURGATED

If the front cover of Capote's novel reveals a convergence between the European avant-garde and American mass culture, then its back cover tells a different story. Reclining on a divan, his right hand resting suggestively below his waist, Capote stares intently at his beholders—a pose that belongs to a tradition of gay male authors displaying themselves that originated with Whitman's open collar on the fly-leaf of *Leaves of Grass*. Putting Capote on the back cover was savvy marketing. "This book," observed editors at New American Library (NAL) in their internal memoranda in the lead-up to publishing Capote's *A Tree of Night* (1949), "should be tied in as closely as possible with OTHER VOICES, OTHER ROOMS and with this spectacular young author himself." A tie-in seemed like a good idea because Capote was considered "exotic," and "his widely reproduced picture" promised "a good many newsstand sales." However, Capote himself wanted something different, newsstand sales be damned. "As for the book," he wrote to Victor Weybright, NAL publisher, "I hope the jacket will be plain—That is, not so gaudy as the one used on OTHER VOICES. I would prefer, too, that you did not have a photograph of me . . . the biography, I think, should be simply that I was born in New Orleans and have published 3 books."[28]

In the previous chapter, we suggested that the book cover is a medium in the sense of being a mediator or intermediary: it brings people together and brokers their relationships to one another. This does not mean, however, that the people who work on book covers always get along. The history of the book cover is also the history of feuds among writers, editors, agents, publishers, and designers. J. D. Salinger, for example, was so dismayed by the cover of the 1953 Signet/NAL paperback of *The Catcher in the Rye* (see page 112) that he insisted on his own design for the Bantam cover of *Nine Stories*. Salinger asked Weybright not to show protagonist Holden Caulfield's face. Like Franz Kafka, who wanted no insect on the cover for *The Metamorphosis*, and like Vladimir Nabokov, who hated the idea of *Lolita* being covered with an image of a young girl, Salinger could not accept a visual representation of his main character. But NAL's cover designer James Avati—widely known as "the Rembrandt of Paperbacks"—had a different plan in mind: "Let us show [Holden] coming down Broadway or Forty-Second Street expressing his pained reaction to people who LIKE movies, etc."[29] The final image, perhaps as a slight concession to Salinger, has Holden walking away from us at a different kind of "lure": what appears to be a Times Square strip club and a man soliciting a prostitute.

Just as they do today, paperback publishers in the mid-twentieth century printed books in multiple genres: new literary novels, reprints of classic literature, serious nonfiction, racy pulp fiction, whodunits, horror, fantasy, and so on. To glance at this archive of covers, then, is to see a mixed bag of styles—high and low and everything in between. On the one hand, there were "quality paperbacks," which emerged after Jason Epstein launched Anchor Books in 1953 and Knopf launched Vintage in 1954. (Beacon and Meridian soon followed.) Many Anchor titles came with covers by Edward Gorey (see page 111), and they sold especially well. On the other hand, there was plenty of raunchy, exploitative, or otherwise problematic imagery. A famous example is the so-called nipple cover, attributed to a prolific pulp artist named Rudolph Belarski, whose design appears on the 1948 paperback reprint of a 1925 novel called *The Private Life of Helen of Troy*. While the novel itself makes no references to breasts, save for one mention of a "bosom," its cover suggests otherwise. Belarski claimed that paperback publishers did not care if the scene he depicted was in the novel. "The editors would say, 'Don't worry, we'll just *write* it in.'"[30]

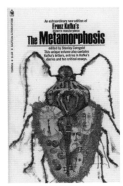

Opposite: The so-called "nipple cover," attributed to a prolific pulp artist named Rudolph Belarski, whose design appears on the 1948 paperback reprint of a 1925 novel called *The Private Life of Helen of Troy* by John Erskine.

Kafka explicitly stated that he didn't want a bug on the cover of this book.

404 SIX SURVIVED TO TELL WHAT HAPPENED

HIROSHIMA

John
Hersey

A BANTAM BOOK
Complete and Unabridged

Four covers by Edward Gorey for Doubleday/Anchor Books, where he worked from 1953 to 1960.

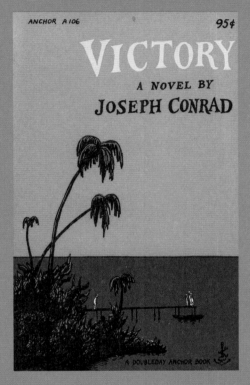

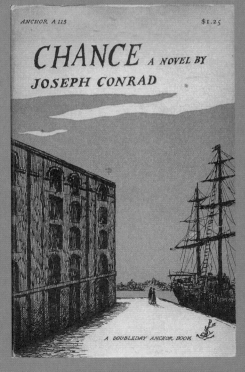

Paperback covers misrepresented the text in other ways, too. Take, for example, Bantam Book No. 404: John Hersey's *Hiroshima*. Originally published in the August 31, 1946, issue of the *New Yorker*, *Hiroshima* recounts what the magazine's editors called, in a statement to readers of the issue, "the almost complete obliteration of a city by one atomic bomb." Within a few months *Hiroshima* was brought out as a hardback book, with a subdued, text-based cover that leads us to assume, rightly, that *Hiroshima* takes place in Hiroshima. The cover of the Bantam paperback, however, implies a different setting. In this image, two people, not Japanese, are fleeing an explosion just beyond the frame. They are young, white, and stylish: she epitomizes New Look fashion in her loafers and gathered skirt, and he sports pleated cuffs and a fitted trench coat—the same type of coat that Holden dons on the cover of the 1953 Signet/NAL paperback of *The Catcher in the Rye*. Bantam Book No. 404, it appears, takes place in America.

The cover designer, Geoffrey Biggs, wasn't trying to be deceptive. As he says, in a note that sits just before the copyright page, he was trying to be universal: "I just drew two perfectly ordinary people—like you or me—and had them portray alarm, anxiety, and yet wild hope for survival as they run from man-made disaster in a big city—a city like yours or mine." By some dubious logic of substitution, as the six Japanese survivors in Hersey's narrative become two white ones on the cover, an actual act of war becomes merely a possible one. Within a few years, perhaps seeking a better detail to carry the metaphoric weight of the book, Bantam discontinued Biggs's cover, replacing it with an image that includes an official photograph of a mushroom cloud.

In the 1970s, Penguin UK continued to publish notable book covers, including iconic designs by David Pelham for novels such as Anthony Burgess's *A Clockwork Orange* and S. Neil Fujita's cover for Truman Capote's *In Cold Blood* (see page 78). The publishing industry in the United States began a process of consolidation, which changed the conditions for both paperback and hardcover book design. Through mergers and acquisitions, large corporations were formed. While independent publishers, such as Grove and New Directions, still nurtured innovative work, they were overshadowed by big houses that were beginning to act like the powerful

Catcher in the Rye by J. D. Salinger, 1953, cover design by James Avati.

"I had to create this image in one night. When Stanley Kubrick unaccountably refused to supply us with promotional press shots, I immediately commissioned a well-known illustrator to help out. The result was not only unacceptable but it was also inexcusably late, so we were horribly out of time . . . I had a very clear image in my mind's eye as to how the cover should look, and so, collecting up a few supplies from the art department, I sped home to my Highgate flat to create the cover myself. I remember a motorcycle messenger arriving at 4:30 a.m. to deliver the 'repro.' Another messenger arrived at 7 a.m. to whisk the artwork off to the printer. Consequently, I had not had time to properly scrutinize the image, to make the small adjustments and refinements that I still believe it needed. So now, every time I see that image, all I see are the mistakes. But then, maybe it's those unfinished rough edges that contribute to its appeal. Who knows?"
—David Pelham on his cover for *A Clockwork Orange* by Anthony Burgess (*right*)

ANTHONY BURGESS

A CLOCKWORK ORANGE

Paul Bacon and the "big book look." *Saint Jack* by Paul Theroux, 1973, cover design by Paul Bacon.

media conglomerates that they are today.[31] The effect was a lot of bland cover art. "The playfulness of Rand and the spontaneity of Kuhlman," write Ned Drew and Paul Sternberger, "gave way to the more distanced, cooler sensibility of sanitized corporate programs. The mythic designer-as-artistic-creator was waning in favor of a more professionalized designer who could be an effective cog in the gears of the corporate machine."[32]

Paul Bacon was a designer who stood out during this time. Bacon pioneered what is known as the "big book look," which is today the default look for high literary fiction and serious nonfiction. (It's also a safe choice for a controversial text.) Examples include his jackets for Joseph Heller's *Catch-22*, Meyer Levin's *Compulsion*, William Styron's *The Confessions of Nat Turner*, E. L. Doctorow's *Ragtime*, and Paul Theroux's *Saint Jack*. Unlike many other cover designers, Bacon read the manuscripts that he was assigned, rather than just their synopses, which enabled him, in turn, to develop subtle interpretations of the author's ideas, without imposing his own vision too forcefully. "I'd always tell myself," Bacon said, "'You're not the star of the show. The author took three and a half years to write the goddamn thing and the publisher is spending a fortune on it, so just back off."[33]

By the end of the 1970s, book covers began to exhibit features that would come to be seen as characteristically Postmodern. The Vintage Contemporaries series, designed by Lorraine Louie, provides an excellent example of this aesthetic, which reached its climax as desktop publishing was becoming more widespread. As in Goldberg's cover for *Ulysses*, Postmodernist design tends to employ pastiche and to be conscious of its relationship to historical sources. Much of this design is disjunctive, collagelike, and purposefully vague and complex, and it tends to use a familiar typeface such as Kabel. In addition to Goldberg's work, covers by April Greiman, Dan Friedman, Lorraine Wild, Fred Marcellino, Michael Ian Kaye, and Paula Scher exemplify Postmodernism.

Some of this work—particularly that associated with the Cranbrook Academy of Art and the design magazine *Emigre*—was highly theoretical, informed by the writings of radical thinkers such as Jacques Derrida, Jean-François Lyotard, and Guy Debord. In general, Postmodernist philosophy is skeptical of "grand narratives" and stable meanings, and aware of the chasm between reality and representation in a society beset by media images. Postmodernist designers aimed to express these ideas in visual terms—to enact the contingency of meaning or the unfettered flow of images into one another. If this makes these designers sound like prophets of digital culture, they were not always greeted with open arms. Rand lived long enough to decry the rise of Postmodernism. Massimo Vignelli, another Modernist, attacked *Emigre* for its promotion of hyper-intellectual design for designers. And critic Steven Heller called this work "deceptively conceptual, when in reality the pseudo-poetic imagery camouflages the fact of a nonexistent point of view."[34]

So where are we now? As in literature and other arts, Postmodernism receded into the background during the 1990s and early 2000s. The waning of Postmodernism brought, as art critic Hal Foster puts it, "the return of the real" in visual art: that is, the return of art grounded in the material conditions of actual bodies and social sites.[35] Meanwhile, Amazon became successful enough to go public in 1997, and new design tools emerged: Quark XPress, Adobe InDesign, and Adobe Illustrator. These two developments—the decline of Postmodernism and the rise of digital technology and culture—have defined cover art in our time. If, as Nietzsche famously proclaimed, our writing tools shape our thoughts, then our design software shapes how our thoughts look.[36] The affordances of a particular design tool make themselves visible in the trends that characterize cover design in a particular season, year, or historical moment.[37]

Still, the most interesting designers, rather than being slaves to their technology, know how to work both *with* and *against* new tools and the trends that they help to inspire. Building on the tradition started by its founder, for instance, Knopf has nurtured some of the most inventive cover design over the years, beginning in 1987 with the arrival of Sonny Mehta (as editor in chief) and Carol Devine Carson (as art director). Together, Mehta and Carson created a climate in which many talented designers could thrive. Many other imprints—Penguin Press, Scribner, Farrar Straus & Giroux, Little Brown, Doubleday, Viking, and others—also foster good design

J O Y
WILLIAMS

TAKING
CARE

"Hypnotic...one of our most remarkable
storytellers."
—ANN BEATTIE

VINTAGE
CONTEMPORARIES

CORMAC
McCARTHY

SUTTREE

"Perhaps the closest we have to a genuine heir
to the Faulknerian tradition...his novels
have a stark, mythic quality that is very much
their own." —THE WASHINGTON POST

VINTAGE
CONTEMPORARIES

J A Y
McINERNEY

BRIGHT LIGHTS,
BIG CITY

"A rambunctious, deadly funny novel that goes
right for the mark—the human heart."
—RAYMOND CARVER

VINTAGE
CONTEMPORARIES

My conviction is that [prior to the creation of Vintage Contemporaries (VC)] publishers paid far too little attention to what's obviously the most important aspect in presenting a book to a largely disinterested public. Covers simply weren't a priority, or else were subject to mediocre taste or none at all. Certainly, uniform designs were common in Europe by then, and since VC was a new program altogether, I wanted people to identify books in a series that included highly regarded writers—[Peter] Matthiessen, [Raymond] Carver, etc.—with ones unfairly overlooked in my view—[Thomas] McGuane, [James] Crumley—and such newcomers as [Jay]

"The artist, Marc Tauss, managed to capture something essential about the book. The image had just the right degree of specificity. If the young man's face were visible, his expression discernible—that would have over-determined the image."
—Jay McInerney, author of *Bright Lights, Big City*

Postmodernism in cover design. *Opposite:* Lorraine Louie's series look for Vintage Contemporaries. *This page:* Carin Goldberg's covers for Kurt Vonnegut.

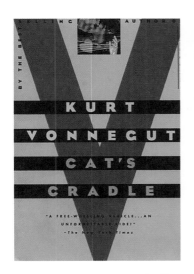

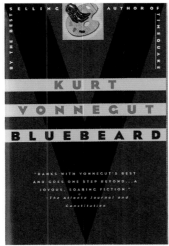

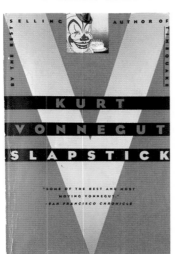

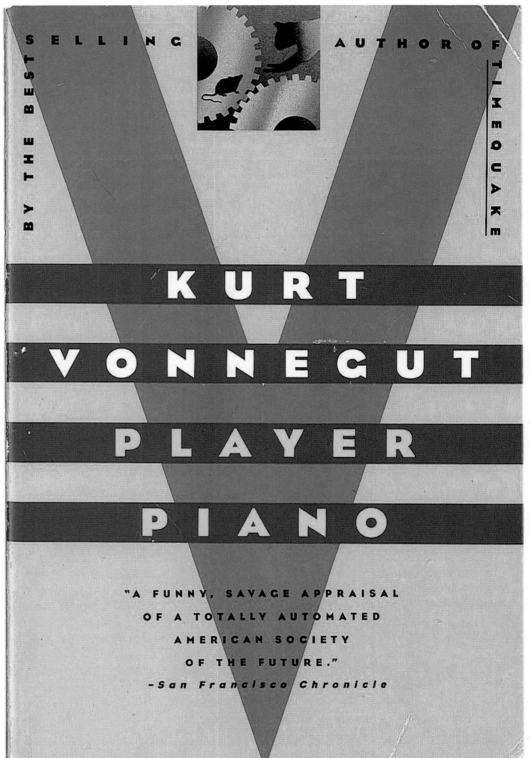

within corporate environments, which can be restrictive and necessarily focused on sales. Likewise, smaller operations—such as New Directions, Graywolf, Tin House, Catapult, Verso, and Ugly Duckling Presse—support innovative cover design, as do university presses such as Harvard, Duke, Princeton, and Chicago. And then there's Fitzcarraldo Editions, an independent publisher of contemporary fiction and long-form essays, which specializes in covers that are, essentially, anti-covers. Avoiding illustration, they employ text only: white lettering against a blue background for fiction and the reverse for essays. While these covers are striking, they achieve their effects without relying on either visual imagery or the (seemingly) hand-drawn lettering so prevalent in cover design today. Persephone Books produces imageless covers in much the same fashion, as does Penguin's Black Classics series.

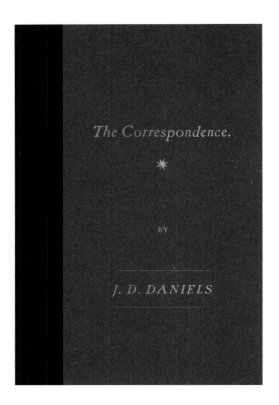

Not all readers have welcomed the rise of the anti-cover. Sarah McNally, owner of the independent bookstore McNally Jackson in New York City, confessed, "I used to wish that American publishers made simple, text-only book covers, like the French do, but then my bookstores started selling Fitzcarraldo editions. They were all I had hoped for, and I realized that I hadn't actually wanted what I'd thought I'd wanted. As a bookseller and as a reader I found them obfuscating. I wanted cues."[38] McNally's point is that a cover image can convey—in an instant—all you need to know about what kind of book you're dealing with. "You can guide your judgement of an apple by its skin," she continued, "and likewise you can guide your judgement of a book by its cover." While minimalist covers make for an appealing foil to the relentless stream of information, imagery, and detritus within digital culture, they are perhaps too plain for consumers seeking a lightning-fast download of all the pertinent facts about a book.

All told, then, the emergence of digital culture has forced designers to become incredibly inventive in order to attract the attention of a shrewd online viewership. These days, the process of buying books usually begins with Google and ends with Amazon; half of all book purchases in the United States are made through that online retailer, and cover design reflects this trend. The splashy prints and blocky text found on many contemporary covers look stunning on even the smallest of screens. However, it's also true that the physical book has attained new status: it feels more precious, as a material thing with texture and heft, than it did during the middle of the twentieth century. Since 2013, print book sales are up by 11 percent. Meanwhile, amid the decline of Barnes & Noble and other corporate chains, the independent bookstore is flourishing. Indies increased by 35 percent between 2009 and 2015, according to the American Booksellers Association.[39]

Fatigued by screen time, it seems, we fetishize the boutique experience of strolling the aisles of expertly curated titles, touching and smelling books. The possibility of losing the book as a material object has made us all more sensitive to its look and feel. Cover designers, therefore, must be nimble in creating designs that will not only play well on mobile devices and social media but also provide a satisfying experience IRL. How do they create such designs? We answer this question most fully in chapter five. But first, we explore what the book cover does as a medium of art, design, and literary interpretation.

The Complete
Plain Words

Sir Ernest Gowers

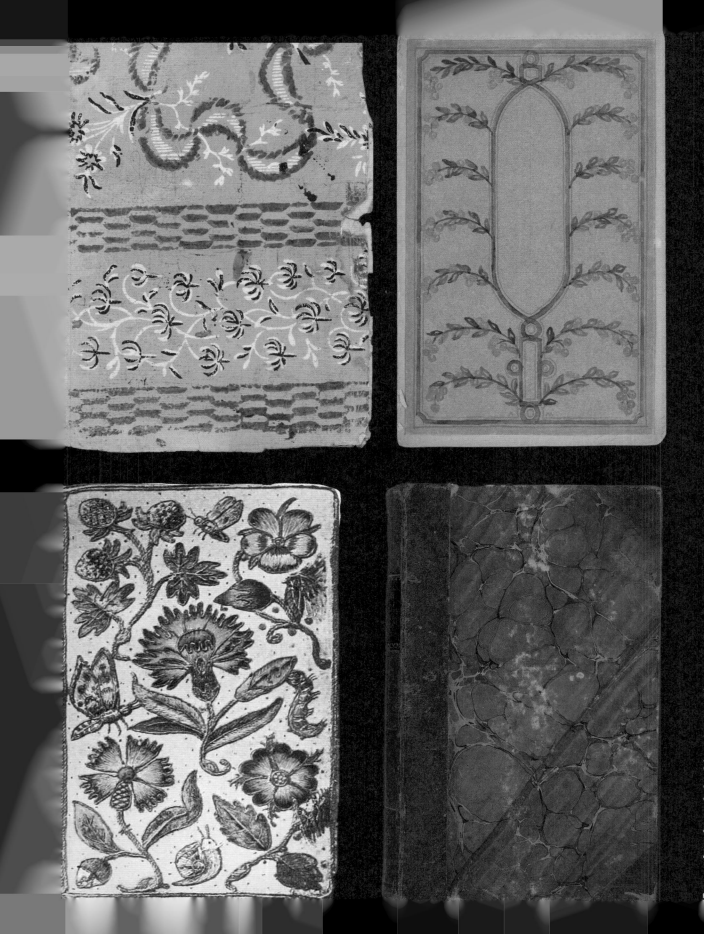

In my decades of dealing books I've never encountered a pre-twentieth century jacket that suggested any purpose beyond either protecting the book beneath it or to offer a modest decorative element to the object being offered for sale." —Glenn Horowitz, bookseller

Some early book coverings. *Opposite, clockwise from left:* A sidewall fragment repurposed as a book cover; a gouache book cover; a leather-bound, marbled cover; an embroidered cover. *This page:* A nineteenth-century slipcase.

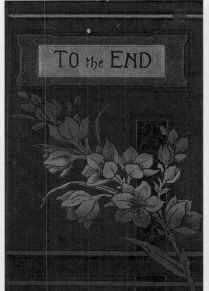

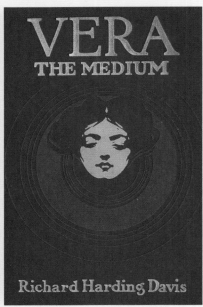

The Yellow Book

An Illustrated Quarterly

Volume III October 1894

Price $1.50 Net

London: John Lane
Boston: Copeland & Day
SECOND EDITION

Price 5/- Net

MY GARDEN IN AUTUMN AND WINTER

TO the END

THE FEET

VERA
THE MEDIUM

Richard Harding Davis

Clockwise from left: A Masque of Days by Charles Lamb, 1901, design by Walter Crane. The Yellow Book, Volume III, 1892, cover by Aubrey Beardsley. Vera, the Medium by Richard Harding Davis, 1908. The Feet, 1871. To the End, 1898. My Garden in Autumn, 1914, cover by Katherine Cameron. Opposite: Too Curious, 1888.

Cover design flourished in the Weimar Republic,
and in Soviet Russia during the years between
World War I and World War II. German and Russian
designers employed many of the tropes and techniques
that we think of as distinctly Modern or even
Postmodern: from radical typography and witty
visual juxtapositions to outlandish production
effects and daring colorways and gradients.

John Heartfield's cover
design for *Zement* (*Cement*)
by Feodor Gladkov, 1927.

Architecture of Vkhutemas, 1920–1927
by N. Dokuchaev and Pavel Novitskii,
cover design by El Lissitzky

Pro dva kvadrata (About Two Squares: A Suprematist Tale of Two Squares in Six Constructions), 1922, cover by El Lissitzky Opposite, Clockwise from left: *Kamen': Pervaia kniga stikhov (Stone: First Book of Verse)* by Osip Mandelstam, 1923, cover by Aleksandr Rodchenko. *L'art décoratif et industriel de l'U.R.S.S.*, 1925, cover by Aleksandr Rodchenko. *Selected Verse* by Nikolai Aseev, cover by Aleksandr Rodchenko. "State Planning Committee for Literature, 1925," cover by N. N. Kuprianov.

О. МАНДЕЛЬШТАМ

КАМЕНЬ

ГОСИЗДАТ

L'ART DECORATIF
U.R.S.S.
MOSCOU-PARIS 1925

ЛИТЕРАТУРНЫЙ ЦЕНТР
КОНСТРУКТИВИСТОВ

ГОСПЛАН
ЛИТЕРАТУРЫ

БОРИС АГАПОВ
И. А. АКСЕНОВ
КОРНЕЛИЙ ЗЕЛИНСКИЙ
ВЕРА ИНБЕР
ИЛЬЯ СЕЛЬВИНСКИЙ
Д. ТУМАННЫЙ

СТАТЬИ   СТИХИ

МОСКВА

Н.
А.
С.
е.
е.
в.

THE MODUL

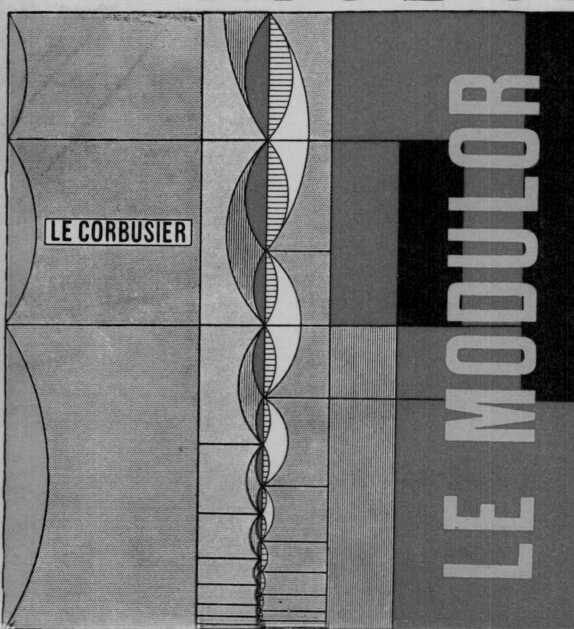

LE CORBUSIER

LE MODULOR

Le Corbusier

The Modulor by Le Corbusier, cover designed by the author. Le Corbusier famously asserted: "Space and light and order. Those are the things that men need just as much as they need bread or a place to sleep." In *The Modulor*, he elaborates a system of measurements used to achieve harmony in architectural compositions, based on the physical dimensions of the average man.

...NIA WOOLF

THE
VOYAGE
OUT

Vanessa Bell's bespoke covers for works by her sister, Virginia Woolf. Bell's work once prompted Woolf to exclaim, "Your style is unique, because so truthful, and therefore it upsets one completely."

...stories which Virginia W...
published during her lifeti...
was *Monday or Tuesday*, a...
that was twenty-two ye...
ago; it has been out of pr...
for many years. Shortly bef...
her death in 1941, she decid...
to prepare a volume of c...
lected short stories wh...
should include most of th...
originally published in *Mon...
or Tuesday* as well as so...
published subsequently...
magazines and some hithe...
unpublished. In the prese...
volume Leonard Woolf h...
attempted to carry out h...
intention : it contains six...
the eight stories in *Monday...
Tuesday*, six stories which a...
peared in magazines betwe...
1922 and 1941, and six whi...
have not previously appear...
in print.

Price 7s. 6d. net.

This Jacket is designed by
Vanessa Bell

Three

...years

the Waves
Virginia Woolf

DALL
VIRGIN

Les parents terribles

Jean Cocteau

*

Examples of how artists have treated the book cover as a medium, blurring the line between art and design. *Opposite:* Henri Matisse's 1940 cover design for the arts journal *Verve*. *This page:* Jean Cocteau's 1955 cover for his *Les Parents terribles*.

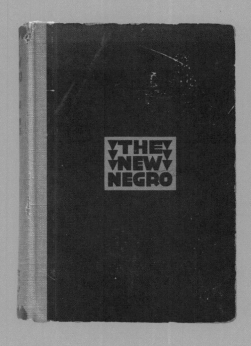

"What can appear least important about the text of blackness— its cover or dust jacket—turns out to reflect nothing less than the ways the black body itself has been figured in the public imagination. Whether suggested by design elements or displayed as representational matter, public perceptions of blackness make their way into negotiations over how a work ought to look when it becomes a book. The end product is not actual flesh, of course, but it is an impression of what Hortense J. Spillers might call the flesh's hieroglyphics—that is, the iconic and spatial qualities we associate with embodied racial subjectivity. Black paratext thus indexes how surrounding every design choice, even those supposedly neutral to race, is a calculation about blackness that puts a body on the line."
—Kinohi Nishikawa, book historian

Aaron Douglas's design for the cover (*right*) and case (*left*) of *The New Negro* anthology, edited by Alain Locke and first published by Albert and Charles Boni in 1925. A key text of the Harlem Renaissance, *The New Negro* draws together black writers, intellectuals, and artists from the era. As an artist, Douglas was a key figure in this movement, and he remains one of the most important cover designers of the twentieth century. Despite the racial inequities of Jim Crow America, he designed important covers for Langston Hughes, Wallace Thurman, Rudolph Fisher, and others.

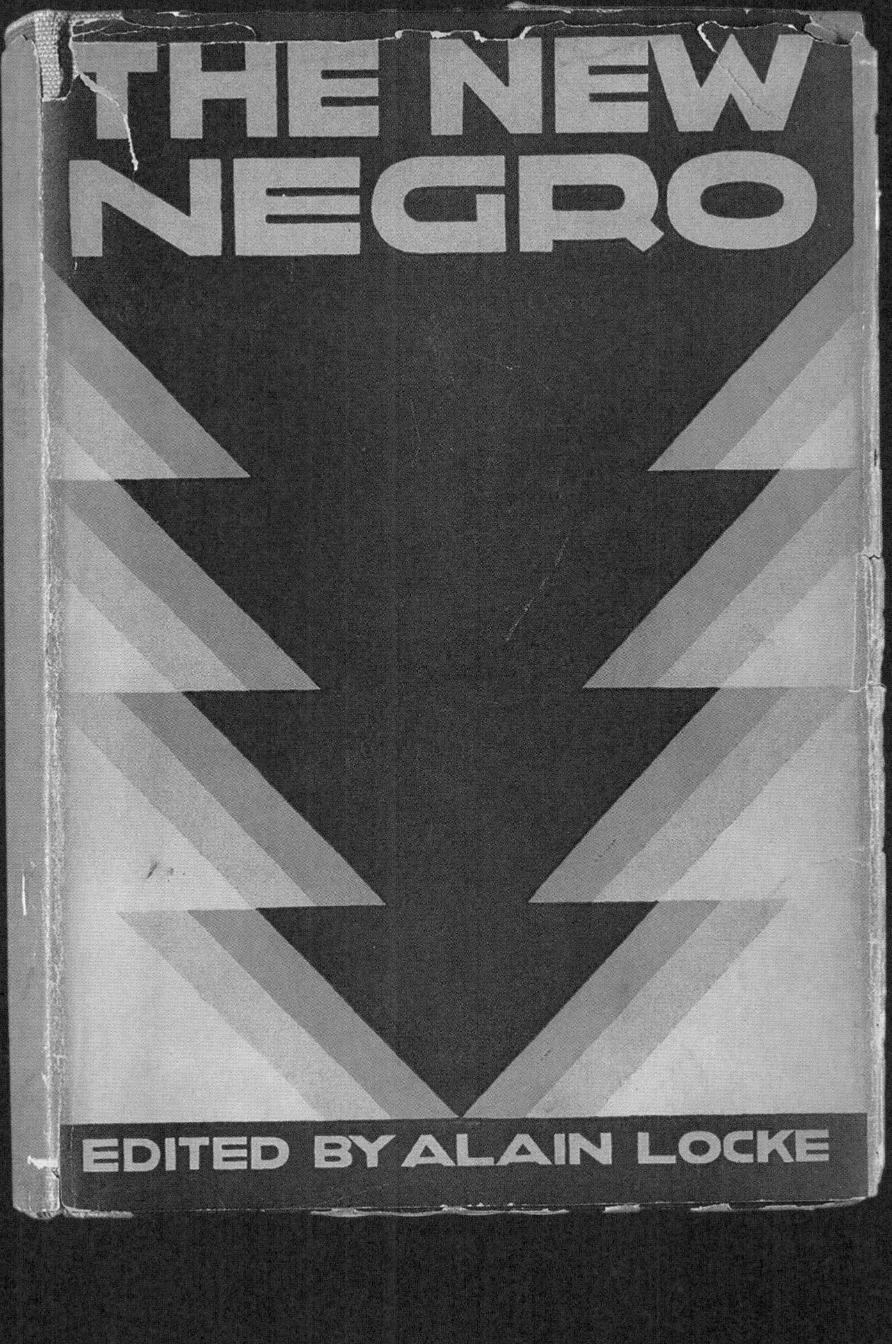
THE NEW NEGRO
EDITED BY ALAIN LOCKE

a new edition of a famous novel with a special
introduction by the author

BRAVE

NEW WORLD

BY ALDOUS HUXLEY

HARPER & BROTHERS ESTABLISHED 1817

E McKnight Kauffer

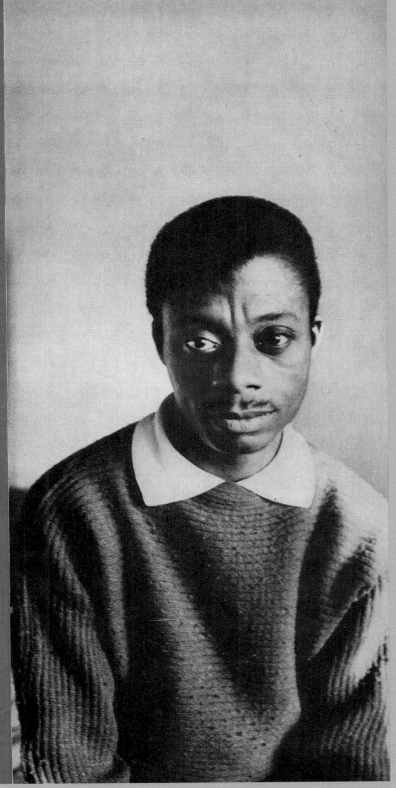

Opposite: E. Michael Mitchell's famous design for *The Catcher in the Rye* By J. D. Salinger, 1951. Mitchell was a close friend of the author. *Above:* The 1991 paperback.

ALBERT CAMUS

CALIGULA
AND 3
OTHER
PLAYS

Giusti

A VINTAGE BOOK · V-207 · $1.45

THE FERVENT YEARS

the story
of the Group Theatre
and the Thirties

1931
1941

1931   1941
by
HAROLD CLURMAN

Paul Rand

FERVENT YEARS

HAROLD CLURMAN

ALFRED A KNOPF

The Wig

The Wig

Charles Wright

The Wig a novel by Charles Wright

author of The Messenger

MILTON GLASER

SOUVENIR
PRESS

Wig by Charles Wright, jacket design by Milton Glaser. Opposite: Bill English's cover for the 1971 Viking Press edition of Jack Kerouac's On the Road, which was originally published in 1957.

a novel
by Jack Kerouac

ON THE ROAD

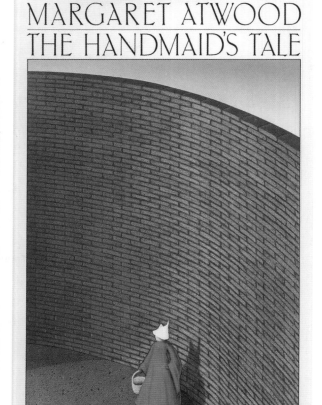

Clockwise from left: *The Fall* by Albert Camus, cover by Mel Calman and Graham Bishop. *The Handmaid's Tale* by Margaret Atwood, illustration by Fred Marcellino. *The Captive Mind* by Czeslaw Milosz, cover by Paul Rand. *Mrs. Wallop* by Peter DeVries, cover by John Alcorn.

T7979 ✳ $1.50 ✳ 🐓 A BANTAM BOOK

In his heart he was not a man, but a wolf
of the steppes. The world-famous
novel of a man's struggle toward liberation.

Hermann
Hesse
Steppenwolf

Steppenwolf by Hermann Hesse, cover by William A. Edwards.

Although it is conventional in the publishing industry for authors and designers to work in separate silos, occasionally, authors have the opportunity to design their own covers, or to be highly involved in the design process. *Above:* Milan Kundera's design for *The Art of the Novel*. *Opposite:* Günter Grass's illustration for *The Flounder*, 1977.

Günter Grass
The Flounder

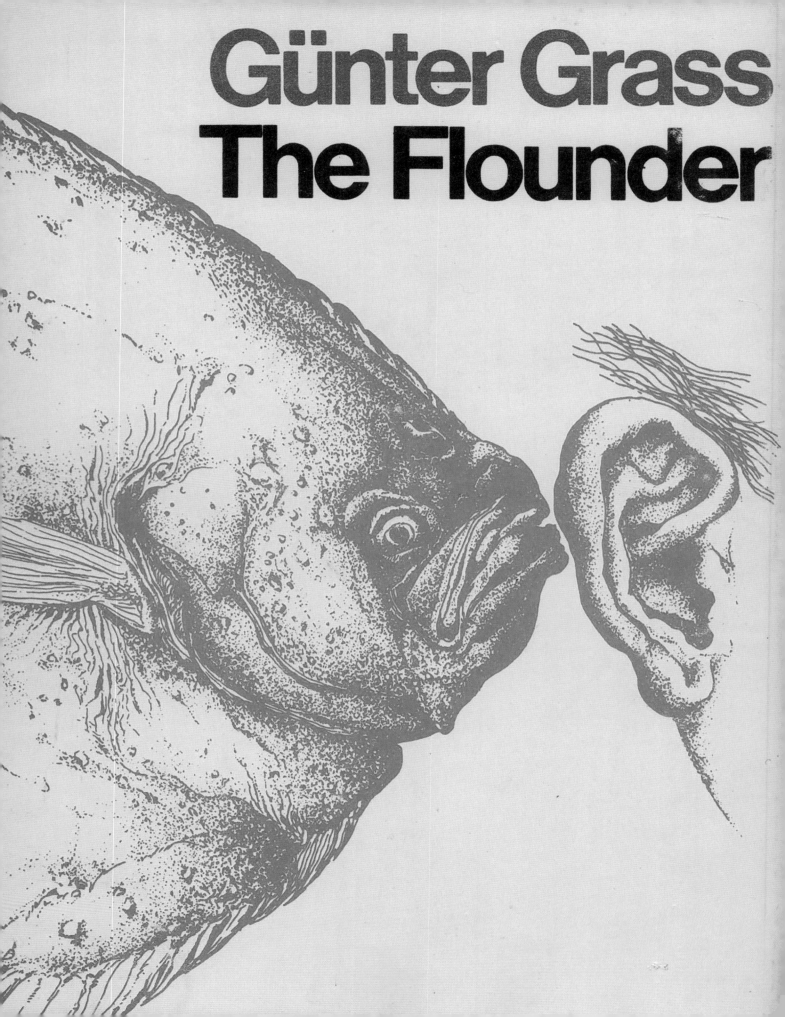

T2341

SIGNET
75¢
BOOKS

Richard Wright

"Wright's unrelentingly bleak landscape was not merely that of the Deep South, or of Chicago, but that of the world, of the human heart." —JAMES BALDWIN

BLACK BOY

A SIGNET BOOK   COMPLETE AND UNABRIDGED

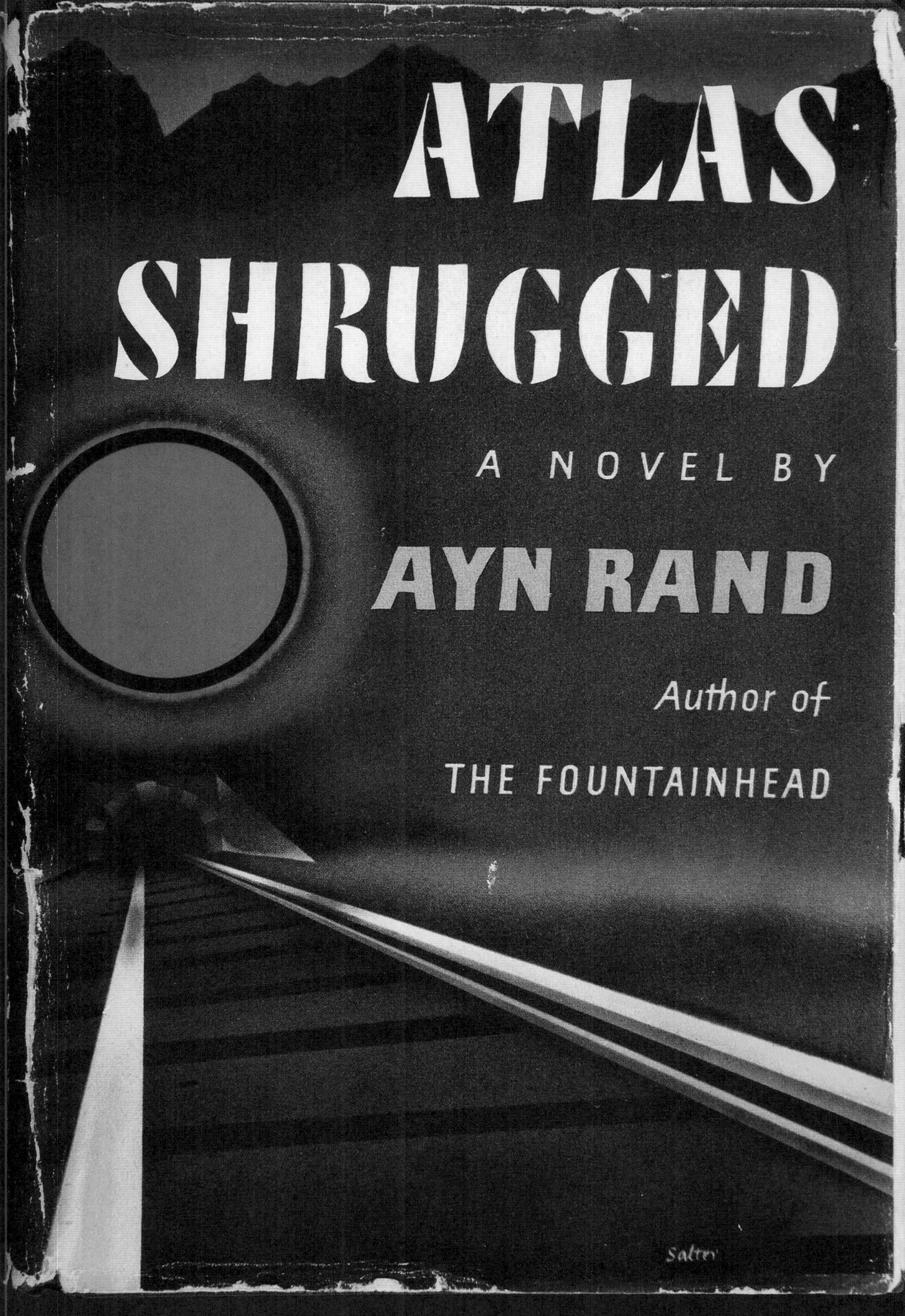

ATLAS SHRUGGED

A NOVEL BY

AYN RAND

Author of

THE FOUNTAINHEAD

Salter

1041

25ᶜ

ERLE STANLEY GARDNER

The Case of the

One-Eyed Witness

A PERRY MASON MYSTERY

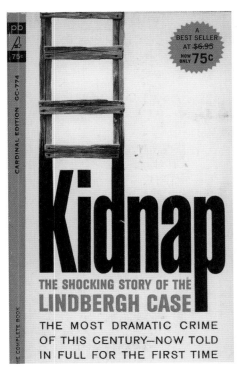

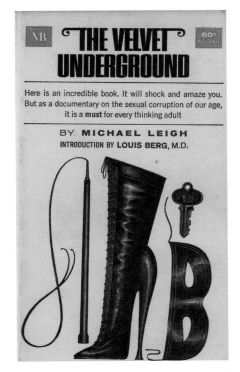

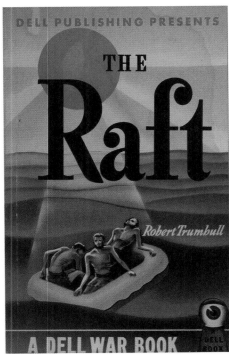

The great age of pulp. *Opposite: The Case of the One-Eyed Witness* by Erle Stanley Gardner, 1955, design uncredited. *This page, clockwise from left: Kidnap* by George Waller, 1962, design uncredited. *The Velvet Underground* by Michael Leigh, 1963, design by Paul Bacon Studio. *Hang-Up* by Sam Ross, 1969, design by George A. Frederiksen. *The Raft* by Robert Trumbull, 1944, design by James Bama.

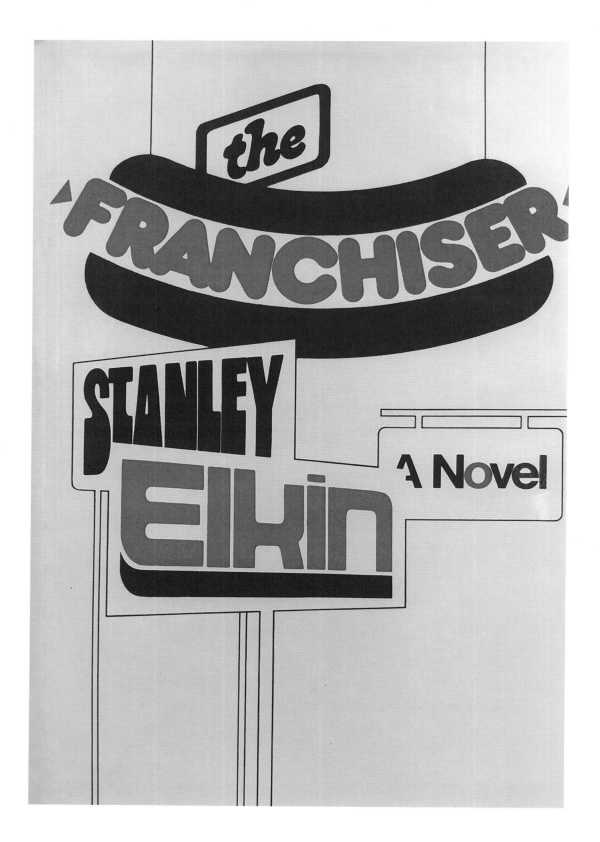

The Franchiser by Stanley Elkin, 1976, cover by Lawrence Ratzkin.
Opposite: The cover that inaugurated the "big book look." *Compulsion* by Meyer Levin, 1956, cover by Paul Bacon.

COMPULSION

a novel by MEYER LEVIN

AN
INNER
SANCTUM
MYSTERY

Ashes
to
Ashes
Emma
Lathen

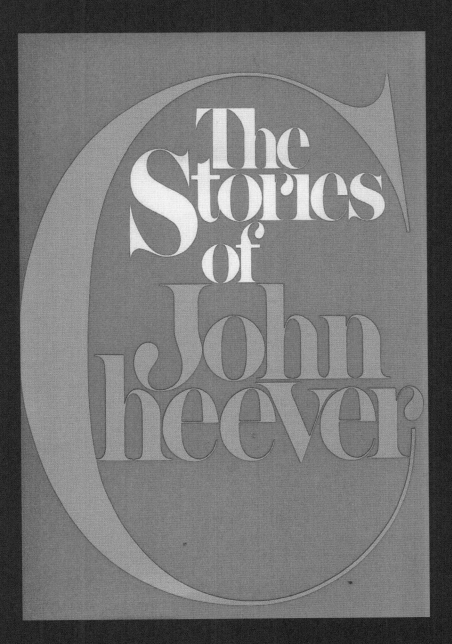

The Stories of John Cheever, 1978, cover by Robert Scudellari. "Sometimes a jacket—like Robert Scudellari's inviting, bright-red wrapper for the very successful 'Stories of John Cheever' (1978), with its huge silver 'C'—does cheer on searchers for a Christmas present to bestow." —John Updike, *New Yorker*

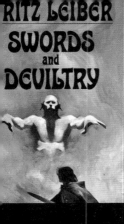

FRITZ LEIBER
SWORDS and DEVILTRY

The Other

THE INVISIBLE MAN
by
H. G. WELLS
one of the greatest science-fiction

SEXUAL POLITICS
A SURPRISING EXAMINATION OF SOCIETY'S MOST ARBITRARY FOLLY
Kate Millett

OF MICE AND MEN

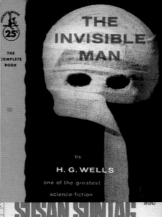

PIERRE OR THE AMBIGUITIES
HERMAN MELVILLE
NABOKOV

H L Mencken

SUSAN SONTAG
AGAINST INTERPRETATION
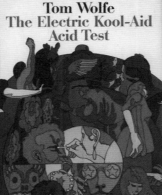

JOHN LE CARRÉ
TINKER, TAILOR, SOLDIER, SPY

Evelyn Waugh

"agencies both beautiful and terrifying"
—The London Times
"The final effect is both chill and comic" He Trans
ansparent
Things

GROUCHO AND ME
The Autobiography of

Tom Wolfe
The Electric Kool-Aid Acid Test

Stronger Than Passion
117 MONARCH BOOKS
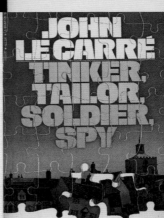

LAFCADIO'S ADVENTURES
a novel

LAST YEAR AT MARIENBAD
text by Alain Robbe-Grillet
for the film by Alain Resnais
with over 140 illustrations
grand prize winner
Venice Film Festival
$3.95

THE **COLOSSUS**

GREEN ORIGINAL

THE TRIAL
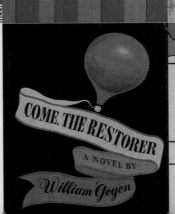

norman MAILER
THE NAKED AND THE DEAD

money
MARTIN AMIS

Axe
Ed McBain
An 87th Precinct Mystery
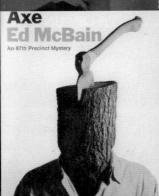

COME, THE RESTORER
A NOVEL BY
William Goyen

Kurt Vonnegut, Jr
BREAKFAST OF CHAMPIONS
A NOVEL

J. Robert Oppenheim

"Great book jacket design prompts a way of looking beyond looking, both by the designer and by the bookshop browser, and creates a pause: a momentary suspension that delivers what Susan Howe has called a 'visual-acoustic shock.' It's a very suggestive shock, with the same ineffable power through which an aroma can conjure a whole world— and it is just as hard to pin down. Synesthesia may explain the conceptual leaps a great book designer makes. Apparently, for some people, synesthesia develops in childhood, when we first deeply engage with abstract ideas. Notable synesthetes include Duke Ellington, Bernadette Mayer, Isaac Newton, Goethe, and [Vladimir] Nabokov (who spoke of 'color hearing' and said, 'I think in images'). In fact, the best designers may have the rarest form of synesthesia—ideasthesia. In any case, they certainly have a sixth sense: like Shirley Jackson, they 'see what the cat sees.'"

—Barbara Epler, editor in chief, New Directions

What the Book
Cover Does

3.

When acclaimed novelist Kazuo Ishiguro received the original US jacket for his 2015 novel, *The Buried Giant*, it was covering a book, although not a book that he had authored. The publisher, Knopf, had sent a prototype of the jacket wrapped around a previously published title. It was not feasible for Ishiguro to review the jacket design via PDF, as is often the case, since the texture of the jacket, which is embossed to mimic the feel of peasants' sackcloth, is a crucial design effect. So when Ishiguro opened his mail, he had the odd experience of *seeing* his own book but *holding* someone else's, which happened to be a novel titled *The Last Werewolf* by Glen Duncan.

The Buried Giant took Ishiguro a long time to write. His wife hated the first draft, composed in 2005, so he put the novel aside and worked on short stories for a while.[40] Like much of Ishiguro's work, *The Buried Giant* achieves profound aesthetic effects, somewhat paradoxically, through soporific declarative prose. "His previous novel, *Never Let Me Go* (2005)," wrote James Wood in the *New Yorker*, "contained passages that appeared to have been entered in a competition called The Ten Most Boring Fictional Scenes."[41] A great many critical adjectives can be used to describe *The Last Werewolf*, but "boring" is not one of them. Bloody, filthy, inane, and puerile, but also at times genuinely gripping and suspenseful, Duncan's novel is nothing if not entertaining.

"Inside the holdall was a second bag made of tough transparent plastic, tightly sealed with tape," explains Jake Marlowe, the narrator of *The Last Werewolf*. "The face had been beaten. At leisure, I imagined. Creases in the plastic held bubbles of blood, as with vacuum-sealed beef in the supermarket."[42] As intensely horrifying as Ishiguro's *Never Let Me Go* can be, it includes nothing quite so lurid and literal minded. Ishiguro's narrators don't often describe blood, and while Marlowe is a fantastical creature, he's no Kathy H. "I am used to the body as a thing separable violently into its constituent parts," Marlowe demurs. "To me a torn-off arm's no more searingly forlorn than a chicken drumstick is to you."[43] For hundreds of years, he's loped the earth with a three-part raison d'être that he calls "fuckkilleat" and that, lately, leaves him beleaguered. "I felt tired, suddenly, weighed down again," he carps. "There's an inner stink comes up at times of all the meat and blood that's passed down my gullet, the offal I've buried my snout in, the guts I've rummaged and gorged on."[44]

Opposite: The Buried Giant by Kazuo Ishiguro, Alfred A. Knopf, 2016, design by Peter Mendelsund. Below: From Ritual to Romance by Jessie L. Weston. The cover design by Leonard Baskin (as well as the book's gnostic, symbolist, and spiritualist subject matter) inspired the cover design for The Buried Giant.

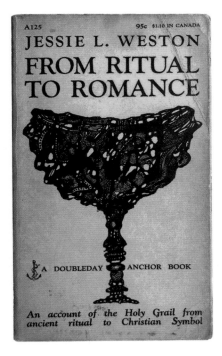

It's unclear whether Ishiguro gorged on this novel, which could be described as the literary equivalent of Halloween candy. But he did thumb the pages, and he liked what he felt and saw. "Well, this is one of the most beautiful jackets ever created," he wrote. "Thank you so much for this . . . with great admiration for your sublime vision." Sublime, perhaps, but also incomplete. Not long after expressing his gratitude, Ishiguro made a pricey request of the publisher: edge staining. This request was inspired by *The Last Werewolf.* To convey a sense of horror—in effect, to dip the book in blood—the edges of *The Last Werewolf* are stained dark red, which rubs off, smearing your fingers as you read about lupine sex and human dismemberment. While Duncan's novel was only intended to serve as a stand-in for Ishiguro's forthcoming book, it nonetheless prompted Ishiguro to ask for a similar edge detail.

The Buried Giant unfolds in a post-Arthurian England that resembles the setting of *Sir Gawain and the Green Knight,* but very little blood is spilled in the novel, so a different, less visceral effect was needed: edges that might suggest not evisceration but the hermetic ancientness of Ishiguro's storyworld. The extensive gold foil stamping on the jacket would have made gilded edges seem like overkill, and deckled page edges just felt trite. Black staining on the edges, however, especially staining that seems to dissipate as you fan the pages of the book, not only makes the book look old but also captures the atmosphere of a narrative whose protagonists, Axl and Beatrice, must reckon with a pervasive mist, metaphorically if not literally dark, spreading across the land.

Of course, *The Buried Giant* did not have to be packaged this way. But all novels come to us in some packaging or another, and there are both good and bad ways to present a new novel to the world. In the most fundamental sense, this is what the book cover does: it packages and frames the text; it prepares you, both mentally and emotionally, to consume the narrative; and it primes your expectations. The moment you glance at the cover, even if your glance lasts only a second or two, you have entered a transitional zone: a kind of vestibule between text and world, between imaginary and real space. Literary theorists call this zone the "paratext," and there is no question that the paratext has expanded in

the digital age.[45] In the past, it was possible to say that the paratext comprised only the physical book cover, the book jacket, the title page, the copyright page, and other printed matter that appears before the author's text. These days we must include many other elements—Amazon thumbnail images, digital marketing campaigns, merchandise such as tote bags—when we speak of the site where text meets context, where imaginative literature meets reality.

Cover designers work at this site. Their designs are not only advertisements, because books are not merely commodities. Rather, from a potential

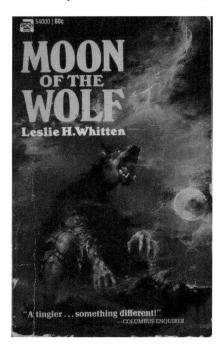

reader's perspective, a good book cover is an invitation to a journey that offers some indication of what it might be like to travel into a given storyworld. This is why it made no sense to splatter *The Buried Giant* in blood. And this is also why, despite the gore that appears in the pages of *The Last Werewolf,* the novel would have been ill served by the sort of werewolf imagery—a seething beast clutching a nubile victim, both dripping in sweat and blood under a full moon—that we associate with the mass-market paperback tradition, since Duncan's novel aims to be more literary and philosophical than much of the work in that tradition.

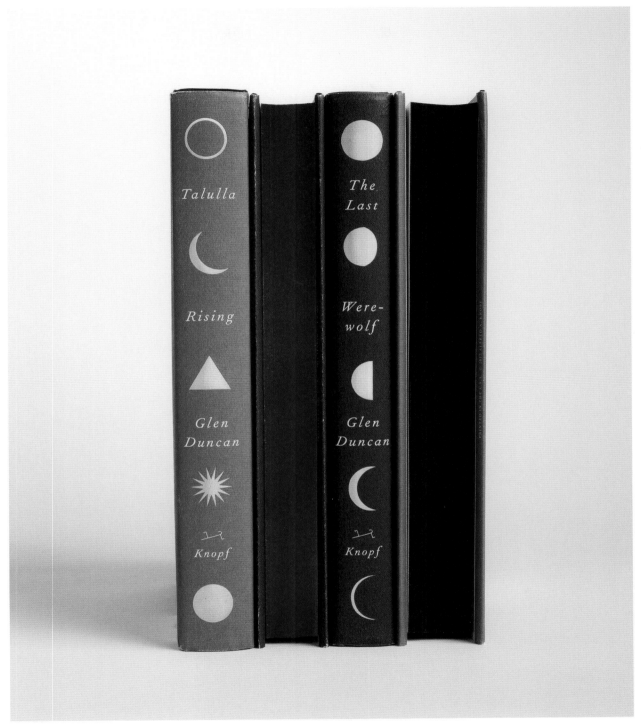

Edge Staining. *The Last Werewolf* and *Talulla Rising* by Glen Duncan, designs by Peter Mendelsund.

"Wendell Minor . . . says when they ask him for a gothic jacket, which traditionally shows an old mansion, a landscape, and a girl in flight, 'I tell them you can have the landscape and the house or you can have the girl. You can't have both. That way at least there's 50 percent chance that I can do something original." —Victor S. Navasky, 1974, New York Times.
Opposite: Moon of the Wolf by Leslie H. Whitten, 1967, cover by George Ziel.

The Voyeur

Alain Robbe-Grillet

Clockwise from left: The Voyeur, Jealousy & In the Labyrinth, and The Erasers by Alain Robbe-Grillet, Grove, 2018, design by Peter Mendelsund.

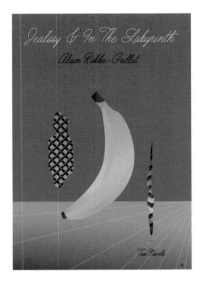

Texts need paratexts as much as we do. As small black marks on a white page, verbal art has very little sensuous content: it's not like painting or music or film, all of which have more immediately perceptible attributes for activating our senses.[46] Painters employ color and shading. Composers can make a crescendo reverberate up your spine. Filmmakers can do both. (Even text messages, for that matter, first catch your eye not because of what they say but because of how they flash.) In a world saturated by information and stimuli, verbal art must be announced to the public in a captivating way, its cover functioning like a carnival barker even when speaking softly. Announcing the text and creating a conduit between imaginary and real space are two key tasks of the book cover. They are what the book cover does, first and foremost, but they are not *all* that it does. The cover's job is not over when you begin reading the pages. A good book cover has that timed-release quality: it changes with you as you read.

Take, for example, the covers that Grove Press commissioned for its republication of novels by Alain Robbe-Grillet. Employing Surrealist motifs that call to mind the work of Salvador Dalí and Luis Buñuel, these covers forge a link between the French *nouveau roman*, for which Robbe-Grillet is known, and the history of visual Surrealism.[47] Rejecting the conventions of plot, character, and theme found in the traditional realist novel, the *nouveau roman* aims to represent the strangeness of lived reality—unencumbered by the ordering devices of literature and culture. "At every moment," Robbe-Grillet argued, "a continuous fringe of culture (psychology, ethics, metaphysics, etc.) is added to things, giving them a less alien aspect, one that is more comprehensible, more reassuring." He wanted to purge literature of this "fringe," to represent the "stubborn reality" all around us precisely *as it is*, rather than how we have been conditioned to see it. Above all, this meant treating nonhuman objects not as vessels of human significance but as mere objects, whose "surfaces are distinct and smooth, *intact*, neither suspiciously brilliant nor transparent."[48] The Grove Press covers visualize this goal of Robbe-Grillet's by rendering objects and subjects on the same plane, literally situating them on a grid, but providing no obvious logic for how they fit together. Colorful but not brilliant, sharply defined but not transparent, these figures are *just there*. They appear to carry no metaphorical or symbolic meaning. And yet, as a gestalt, each cover opens up the possibility of a different logic, a different ordering principle for reality, perhaps even a Surrealist logic, accessible only in the waking dream-state created by fiction.

Science Fiction
J.G. BALLARD
The Terminal Beach

Penguin Science Fiction covers of *The Terminal Beach*, *The Wind from Nowhere*, and *The Drowned World* by J. G. Ballard, design by David Pelham, who was the art director at Penguin Books between 1968 and 1979.

Science Fiction

J.G.BALLARD

The Drowned World

"I still have some of those early thumbnails, and I notice in the margin of one of them are my notes, quickly scribbled at that meeting and obviously suggested by [J. G.] Ballard. The notes say, 'monumental / tombstones / airless thermonuclear landscape / horizons / a zone devoid of time ....'" David Pelham

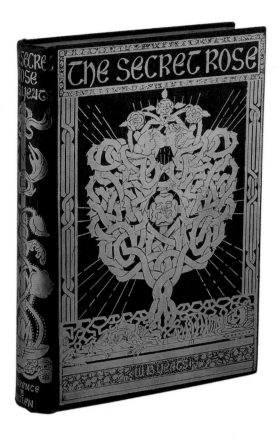

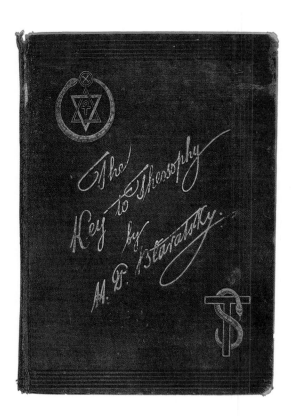

W. B. Yeats, *The Secret Rose*, Mead & Co., 1897.

Helena Blavatsky, *The Key to Theosophy*, 1920.

If the Robbe-Grillet covers function as a kind of literary criticism in visual form, then the cover for Ishiguro's *The Buried Giant* goes a step further in its "reading" of the novel that it presents to the world. Set in sixth- or seventh-century England, just after the end of a war between Saxons and Britons, Ishiguro's novel tells the story of Axl and Beatrice, two elderly married Britons, as they embark on a quest to find their estranged son. In the course of the journey, they encounter two knights: Wistan, a young Saxon warrior, and Sir Gawain, an elderly and slightly clownish nephew of King Arthur. There are adventures with ogres, pixies, dragons, soldiers, and some menacing monks. The most important plot point (that a kind of collective amnesia has

taken hold across the land) and the key theme of the novel (memory and forgetting) are both represented by what Axl and Beatrice call "the mist." Eventually, we learn that "the mist" is the breath of an oppressive she-dragon named Querig, and that the only way to restore the country's stolen memory will be to kill Querig. The novel ends with the vanquishing of Querig and thus the beginning of a new historical epoch in which people will have to confront what they have forgotten, as well as what they have invented to fill in the gaps. It turns out that demystification will have uneven effects. For Axl and Beatrice, it will mean remembering the ups and downs of a love affair; for the Saxons and Britons, collectively, it will mean a return to war. "Who knows

 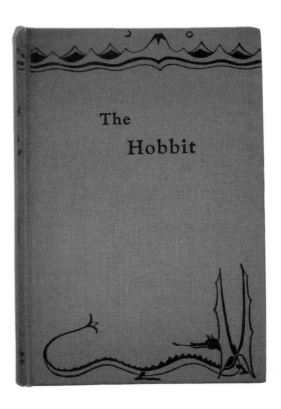

J. R. R. Tolkien, *The Hobbit,* designed by the author, 1937.

what old hatreds will loosen across the land now?" Axl asks. "The giant, once well buried, now stirs."[49]

Elements of this story appear on the book cover. Indeed, successful covers often have a kind of plot, presented visually, that may or may not replicate what's inside the book. The symbols, figures, and calligraphic style of *The Buried Giant* cover were inspired partly by J. R. R. Tolkien's design for the cover of *The Hobbit.* Many of these sketches plunder the iconography of fantasy and folklore; the image of the Holy Grail, the central figure on the finished jacket, was important from the start, as was the map that was commissioned for the book's inside boards, or endpapers. If a book contains a map, it is likely either military history or fantasy—or

Faulkner, which is both. Certain paratextual details, in other words, are indicators of genre: they tell you what kind of book you hold in your hands. Like all abstract categories, genres are imperfect and malleable inventions. No individual work of fantasy perfectly exemplifies the category of fantasy. And no category entirely describes any individual instance of it. However, genres do create a set of more or less durable expectations for readers; we expect epics to feature heroes, love stories to feature lovers, and so on. Book covers *visualize* these expectations. They lay out the terms for engaging with a particular literary artifact, and they make promises or threats about what it might be like to enter the world that the writer has created, whether fictional or factual.

But what happens when jackets violate their own terms, or when books make promises that they don't intend to keep? There is no chalice, no Holy Grail per se, in *The Buried Giant*. The Knopf jacket, in other words, displays an image that never appears in the text—or almost never appears. This image is based on a crucial scene late in the novel, when Ishiguro's narrator describes a sleepy dragon resting in a lair that resembles a rimmed drinking vessel:

Axl helped his wife onto a ledge beside him, then leant over one of the rocks. The pit below was broader and shallower than he had expected—more like a drained pond than something actually dug into the ground. The greater part of it was now in pale sunlight, and seemed to consist entirely of grey rock and gravel—the blackened grass finishing abruptly at the rim—so that the only living thing visible, aside from the dragon herself, was a solitary hawthorn bush sprouting incongruously through the stone near the center of the pit's belly.[50]

This passage gave rise to the map, designed by Neil Gower, that appears on the Knopf hardback's inside boards. For the reader, though, it registers as a kind of ekphrasis: a verbal representation of a visual representation.[51] First you see the book cover and the map, then you read this description of the dragon's lair. What is the relationship between Ishiguro's text and this particular book cover?

Asking this question implies that the meaning of *The Buried Giant* depends partly on the design of its cover. While this might seem like a radical suggestion, since we tend to think that the meaning of a literary text does not involve the look of the book, there is a reason why novelists like Ishiguro are so invested in the aesthetics of their book covers. It is not only that effective covers can drive sales; they also can shape how the text is received before, during, and after the reading period. In the case of *The Buried Giant*, the cover depicts the dragon's lair as the Holy Grail. And this depiction enables us to understand something important about Ishiguro's project. It helps to clarify what is at stake in his engagement with fantasy, which many readers and critics found puzzling. By turning to fantasy, Ishiguro was looking back to the older genres of romance and epic from which emerged the novel as we know it today. As an art form, the novel is both flexible and capacious; it can include everything from Realism to science fiction, werewolf pornography to Arthurian romance. Writing a novel with a dragon as the antagonist, however, Ishiguro ultimately produced a work that perfectly exemplifies neither Realism (which is why Wood called it a "slog") nor fantasy (which is why Ursula Le Guin called it "painful," and said reading it was "like watching a man falling from a high wire while he shouts to the audience, 'Are they going say I'm a tight-rope walker?'").[52] Instead, as Ishiguro has done throughout his writing career, he synthesized the two genres into something new.

This made designing the cover a challenge. In the end, the cover makes two promises about genre— the names "Ishiguro" and "Knopf" suggest literary fiction, while the title, the Holy Grail, and the Tolkienesque figures suggest fantasy—that the text struggles to keep. It also makes one other promise about genre that it keeps perfectly well: for all the boundary blurring that occurs in *The Buried Giant*, it remains a novel. All this is fitting because one of Ishiguro's major themes is the risk of asking for and making promises. "Should Querig die and the mist begin to clear," Axl implores Beatrice. "Should memories return, and among them of times I disappointed you. Or yet of dark deeds I may once have done to make you look at me and see no longer the man you do now. Promise me this at least. Promise, princess, you'll not forget what you feel in your heart at this moment."[53]

Which brings us back to the dragon, who is slain by the knight Wistan in a heroic but subdued climax. What does it mean to kill Querig? This narrative event is full of significance; it can be understood as a metafictional moment, or a moment in which the novel is commenting on the status of fiction itself. Ishiguro, literary novelist, invents a dragon, and the novel as a genre summons the older genres against which it has historically defined itself. Ishiguro, literary novelist, kills a dragon, and the novel then vanquishes those same genres: epic, romance, and fantasy.

But the cover suggests a different reading. If we treat the cover as an interpretation of the text, as all covers are to some degree, then we see that the dragon dies inside a Holy Grail, so when her blood spills, it's the blood of everlasting life. Ishiguro slays genre fiction, but he slays it so that the novel may live forever. To remain culturally relevant, the novel must repeatedly reinvent itself, as it has done since its earliest days. Its dominant mode, Realism, can only remain fresh if it's vigorously challenged by adventuresome writers who push its boundaries, test its limits, and mix it up with other forms of storytelling.

Why would an acclaimed literary author like Ishiguro want to dabble in fantasy? And what explains the rise of literary genre fiction: this emerging hybrid, exemplified by *The Buried Giant* and *The Last Werewolf,* of high-literary writing fused with the conventions of other genres (e.g., fantasy, science fiction, horror) that are often stigmatized as less sophisticated? One answer is that ambitious novelists are seeking new tools to address our current social and political moment. Almost sixty years ago, Philip Roth, a novelist who often explored the boundary between realism and genre fiction, addressed the challenge of representing "reality" in his art. "It stupefies, it sickens, it infuriates," he wrote, "and finally it is even a kind of embarrassment to one's own meager imagination. The actuality is continually outdoing our talents, and the culture tosses up figures almost daily that are the envy of any novelist."[54] Roth could have been writing that in 1969 or 2016 or yesterday. After all, it's not as though reality has gotten any easier to grasp in recent years. In a moment when reality can seem fantastical, conventional Realism might be inadequate to the task of representing the world and presenting universal themes. This is why many novelists are experimenting with new forms of storytelling. It will fall to the cover designers to make these forms legible to potential readers at a glance.

"The actuality is continually outdoing our talents."
—Philip Roth

Left: The Plot Against America by Philip Roth, jacket by Milton Glaser. *Right: The Man in the High Castle* by Philip K. Dick, cover by Jamie Keenan.

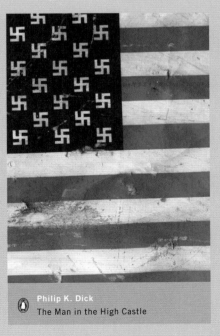

Mass Market
Suspense, Thrillers

1.

4.

5.

2.

3.

6.

1. Large Typography (author, title, or both)
2. Foil Stamping
3. Cover Quote
4. Small Figure, Shadowy Locale, or Artifact
5. Dark Background Color or Gradient
6. All Caps

Literary Fiction

. . . is also a genre. And also, now, legible at a glance. Over the past decade or so, publishers, marketers, art directors, and designers have collaborated to devise an ever-reusable formula for literary fiction jackets. A formula that is as reductive as any other.

1. Large Typography
2. Handmade (though thematically interchangeable)
Elements (decorative patterns, mostly)
3. Bright Colors
4. A Crowding of Space (of primary importance
is that such covers work at tiny sizes on
any digital platform or point of purchase)

The jacket for Stieg Larsson's *The Girl with the Dragon Tattoo* (*opposite*), for instance, might be understood as bearing a closer relationship to the jackets of the aforementioned "literary fiction" genre, (though its design predated the creation of these tropes). It is certainly closer to that than it is to the images and palette of Nordic noir covers on this page.

Genre plays an important role in the look of the book. A key task of the cover designer is to make genre visible by representing an abstract category as a concrete design. Doing so often involves employing the *least intrusive signifier*: the visual emblem that will convey all the requisite information about the contents of the text, without intruding upon the author's vision. While this task might seem as straightforward as putting a blood splatter on the cover of a crime novel or a kissing couple on that of a love story, it can get complicated for a few reasons. First of all, books don't always fit neatly in one genre, and genres are always bending and stretching to accommodate new cultural products. Second, no cover exists in a vacuum, so designers must strike a delicate balance between newness and familiarity. Not every romance can have a kissing couple on the front, or they'd all look the same, even if the kissing couple remains a useful visual cue for the genre at hand. Third, there might be disagreement among the multiple professionals working on a book—author, agent, editor, publisher, marketing executive, publicist, and designer—over how that book should be categorized and marketed. In recent years, moreover, it has become more difficult to differentiate between highbrow literature and genre fiction such as fantasy and horror. These days, werewolves and ghosts roam the halls of Knopf as well as Bantam.

At the same time, many of the most interesting contemporary novels are blurring the boundary between fiction and nonfiction. "Increasingly I'm less interested in writing about fictional people," writer Sheila Heti has proclaimed, "because it seems so tiresome to make up a fake person and put them through the paces of a fake story."[55] To make matters even trickier, visualizing genres doesn't necessarily mean fulfilling our expectations. A book cover must tell you what kind of book you're holding in your hands, and we all carry assumptions about how certain books should look. Many of the most successful covers, however, subvert our expectations. Such covers calibrate accuracy and surprise. They push us to see something in a new way without falsely representing it.

Take, for instance, the Knopf jacket for Stieg Larsson's *The Girl with the Dragon Tattoo* (2008). Bright yellow and featuring a swirling dragon design, this jacket is one of the most iconic in contemporary US fiction. "It was striking and it was different," proclaimed Sonny Mehta, editor in chief at Knopf, which is why he ultimately endorsed it, despite "some push back" from others in the industry.[56] The success of *The Girl with the Dragon Tattoo* elevated the genre of "Nordic Noir" to greater prestige on the world stage; now this genre is widely seen in books, in movies, and on TV. Prior to the appearance of the Knopf *Tattoo* cover, Swedish crime fiction had been marketed globally with several now-familiar cover tropes: snowy landscapes, menacing clouds, blood, chiaroscuro shading, and abstract human figures in various states of anguish, all of

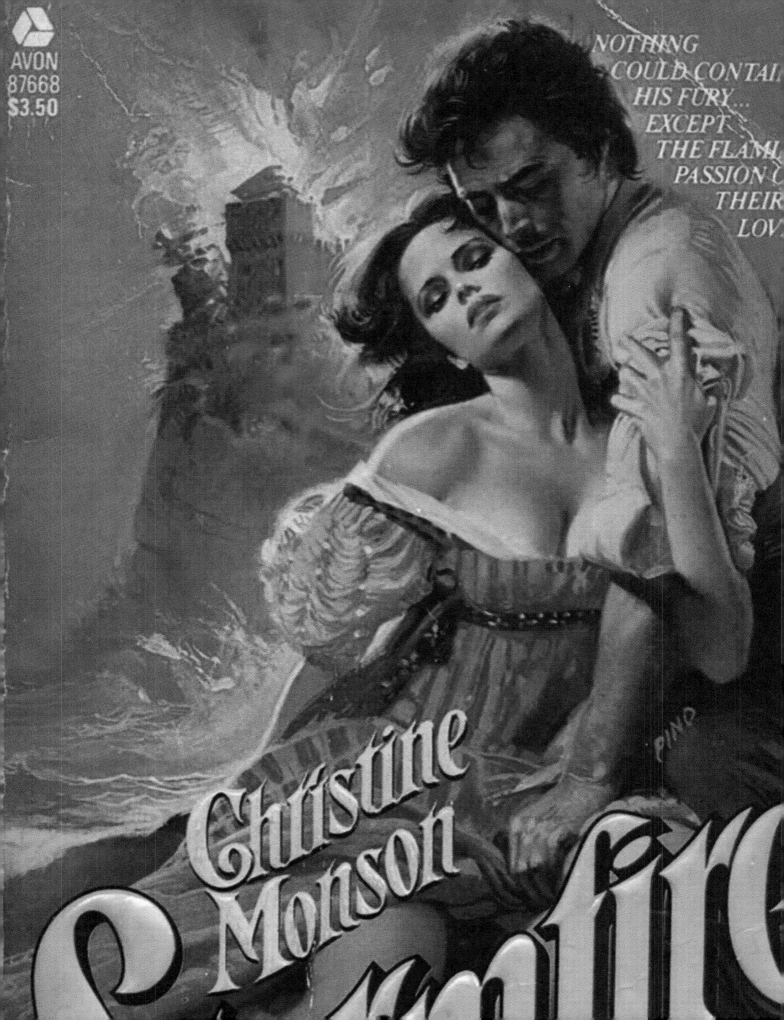

NOTHING
COULD CONTAI
HIS FURY...
EXCEPT
THE FLAM
PASSION (
THEIR
LOV...

Christine
Monson

"You can guide your
judgement of an apple
by its skin ..."
—Sarah McNally,
founder, McNally Jackson
Bookstores

A key task of the cover designer is to make genre visible by representing an abstract category as a concrete design.

Stormfire by Christine Monson, Avon Books, 1984, cover art by Pino Daeni.

which are meant to convey a generalized idea of "The North" as a site of mystery, danger, and extremity.[57] Extending from the tales of Hans Christian Andersen all the way to the "Winter is coming" refrain in *Game of Thrones*, this idea of the north has become a main driver for how fictions of Sweden and Norway are received abroad. The covers of translated novels by Maj Sjöwall and Per Wahlöö, Arne Dahl, Håkan Nesser, Kristina Ohlsson, and Henning Mankell are all good examples of this style of cover design.

In Norway, however, domestic crime fiction is not published with covers that depict snowy landscapes. Local color, it turns out, doesn't matter very much to the locals, which is why, as Jorge Luis Borges averred, "there are no camels" in the Qur'an.[58] Still, whenever domestic literature becomes world literature—that is, whenever a local literary phenomenon becomes a global sensation—it tends to carry the burden of representing the geographical place from which it came. The translation and publication of Swedish crime fiction in well-established foreign series, such as *Actes Sud* in France and *Il Giallo* in Italy, provide a good example of how covers interact with geography and national culture. Indeed, one of the main reasons that a single text usually has multiple covers is that each geographical and national context demands its own style of visual representation. What works well in North America might not work as well in the UK or elsewhere.

The global success of Scandinavian novelists like Larsson and Jo Nesbø raises a more fundamental question: Why crime fiction? Of all genres, why is this one so popular across the globe? On the one hand, there are external forces at play: crime has a lurid appeal, and these books are well marketed and distributed by powerful corporate publishers. On the other hand, there is something internal to the genre that makes it broadly compelling. Invented by Edgar Allan Poe in 1841, with the publication of his short story "The Murders in the Rue Morgue," the modern crime narrative is highly manipulative. First it creates a strong desire to know the truth of the case, then it thwarts this desire for as long as possible, holding us in suspense. Good crime narrative makes us, simultaneously, *want* and *not want* to solve the case: it makes us want to keep on wanting.

A good book cover has the same effect. While covers must accomplish many tasks—packaging the text, creating a link between text and context, visualizing

... it makes us want to keep on wanting.

Three penguins and a gorilla. *Clockwise from left: The Murders in the Rue Morgue* by Edgar Allan Poe, first edition of the photoplay edition, circa 1932. Penguin Crime designs by Romek Marber.

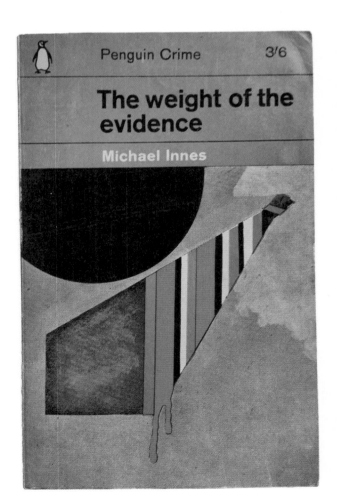

THE MURDERS IN THE RUE MORGUE
AND OTHER TALES OF HORROR

by
EDGAR ALLAN
POE

ILLUSTRATED WITH
SCENES FROM THE
UNIVERSAL
PHOTOPLAY
PRESENTED BY
CARL LAEMMLE

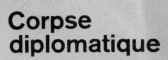

Penguin Crime   3/6

Corpse diplomatique
Delano Ames

Penguin Crime   3/6

The weight of the evidence
Michael Innes

Penguin Crime   3/6

Hangman's holiday
Dorothy L. Sayers

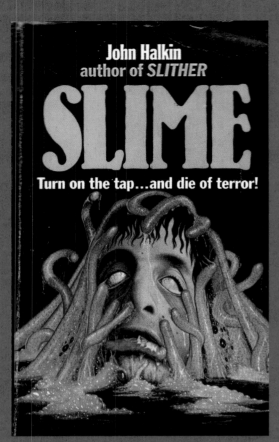

John Halkin
author of *SLITHER*

SLIME

Turn on the tap...and die of terror!

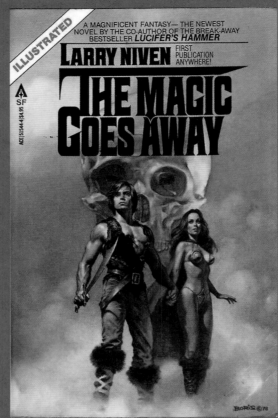

ILLUSTRATED

A MAGNIFICENT FANTASY— THE NEWEST
NOVEL BY THE CO-AUTHOR OF THE BREAK-AWAY
BESTSELLER *LUCIFER'S HAMMER*

LARRY NIVEN
FIRST PUBLICATION ANYWHERE!

ACE 51544/$4.95

THE MAGIC GOES AWAY

BORIS ©78

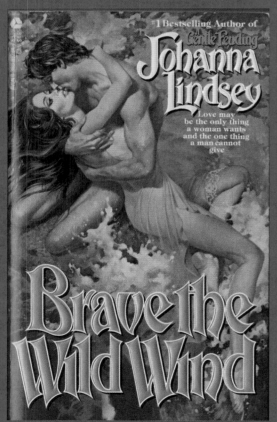

#1 Bestselling Author of
Gentle Feuding

Johanna Lindsey

Love may
be the only thing
a woman wants
and the one thing
a man cannot
give

Brave the Wild Wind

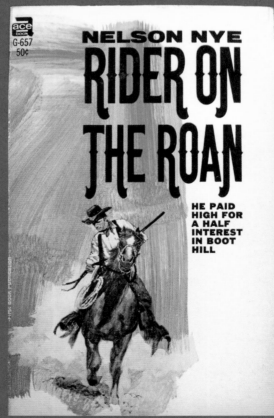

ace book
G-657
50¢

NELSON NYE

RIDER ON THE ROAN

HE PAID
HIGH FOR
A HALF
INTEREST
IN BOOT
HILL

Panther Science Fiction

asimov
Second Foundation

586 01713 5

Classic genre signals. Sci-fi (*Second Foundation* by Isaac Asimov, cover illustration by Chris Foss, 1976). Opposite, clockwise from left: Horror (*Slime* by John Halkin, cover artist unknown, 1984), fantasy (*The Magic Goes Away* by Larry Niven, cover art by Boris Vallejo, 1976), western (*Rider on the Roan* by Nelson Nye, cover art by Gerard McConnell, 1967), and romance (*Brave the Wild Wind* by Johanna Lindsey, cover painting by Robert McGinnis, 1984).

The "least intrusive signifier" is what we call the figure that enables a designer to sig-nal genre while not crowding out other forms of design. In the case of the cover below, for Jo Nesbø's *The Snowman* (cover design by Peter Mendelsund), the single blood drip performs all of the heavy lifting to telegraph genre to a potential audience.

"Least instrusive signifier"

Of course, cover design tropes for various genres are not static, and as a genre's reception and audience changes, its cover vernaculars do as well.

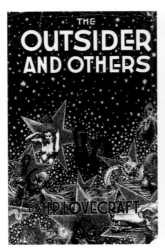

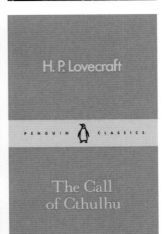

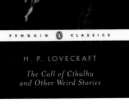

genres, navigating the challenges of different visual cultures across the globe—their most important job is to make you long to read the book, without revealing too much about its contents. It is an added bonus if, as in the case of *The Buried Giant,* the cover changes with you as you read, offering its own interpretive lens on the text at hand.

There is no doubt that digital technology is changing the way that we read and consume books, which means, in turn, that the work of the book cover is changing too. In today's book culture, covers must work simultaneously as clickable thumbnails and sensuous, artful objects. They must be as enticing to the distracted online shopper as they are to the deliberative buyer at the local bookstore. For a while it seemed as though online retail would destroy independent bookstores, but such stores are thriving again—it turns out that we still love the immediacy of seeing and touching and smelling the physical book. (To be sure, new book smell is the bibliophile's version of new car smell.) And while there are many reasons to criticize Amazon and other online retailers, it is worth remembering that Amazon started as a bookstore. According to author and journalist Brad Stone, Jeff Bezos had the idea for his company after reading Ishiguro's *The Remains of the Day.*[59] Love it or hate it, online retail has made the visual culture of books more important than ever, but it has simultaneously imposed new design constraints on cover art. We discuss those constraints in chapter five, but first we need to consider how and why the book cover has taken on new social and cultural significance in our time.

"Book covers, to me, serve all kinds of functions, though probably the reason I like them most is just for pleasure's sake. If it's a book I don't know, the cover gives me a sense of what the atmosphere of the book might be like, almost like a little tone poem. For books I've already read and loved, the cover becomes part of my experience of the book, like my emotional attachment to a familiar cover from childhood. I've always been jealous of artists and their tools, their paintbrushes and cameras and drawing pens. Writers don't get to use anything fun: they have to work with words, the most basic of all tools, the same tools that constitute the nonsense that arrives in your spam box all day. Book covers give me that little pressure release from the ubiquity of words. They link writing to the visual, and, when they're good, covers also elevate the words inside to the level of art, or at least indicate to the reader that this is a different reading experience than reading your emails."
—Emma Cline, author of *The Girls*

"In the end, nobody buys a book jacket."
—John Updike, *New Yorker*

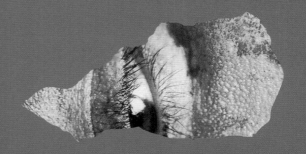

Why the Book
Cover Matters

4.

Any discussion of why the book cover matters must begin by acknowledging its contradictory status.

On the one hand, the book cover is just another fleeting image in a dizzying visual culture; on the other hand, it's a strange and special kind of image, unlike any other, whose meanings and functions depend on the circumstances of display and viewership. Some might say book covers are trivial things, unnecessary at best, distracting and off-putting at worst. As mass-produced objects, they lack the aura of singularity that we associate with fine arts such as painting and sculpture. Nevertheless, book covers are important, both within literary culture and beyond. Authors, agents, and editors want their books represented accurately and beautifully. Designers want their work to stand out as original and striking. Publishers want book covers that gin up publicity and lead to sales. And readers, of course, are not just readers, but also people who use books in all sorts of ways beyond the obvious—to decorate homes, to populate social media, and to display their taste, lifestyle, and personal brand. Like pictures of food, clothing, or tropical beaches, Instagram "shelfies" reveal a little of who you are or hope to be.

Book covers are, in this sense, images that construct an image: the image of you, your interests and desires, your thoughts and feelings, your cultural, social, and political identity. And as images, they can and do circulate widely across media platforms and channels. We know a book cover has become truly iconic when it leaps from the literary realm to the world of fashion, when it's emblazoned on a tote bag or a T-shirt. Such covers seem to have lives of their own. Untethered from the book, they no longer perform many of the functions that we discussed in the previous chapter, but instead serve primarily as vehicles for self-expression.

What is an image? The notion is an ancient one, dating all the way back to the classical Greek idea of *opsis* as explained in Aristotle's *Poetics*. Honed over the years by philosophers, a basic definition of an image is a sign or symbol of something by virtue of sensuous resemblance.[60] An image of a Christmas tree, for example, strikes the eyes in much the same way that an actual tree does; for the perceiver, its color, texture, and shape mimic those of the Fraser fir in the forest. But what does a book cover mimic? This question is not easily answered. Unless it's text based, a book cover does not sensuously resemble the printed pages that it contains. And when a book cover does depict something tangible—a human figure, a snowy field, a creature, a weapon—it's pointing not only to an object in the world (like a tree in the forest) but also to an object that resides somewhere else: in the mental space of the designer as it has been shaped, momentarily, by the words of the author.

Book covers are, in other words, ambiguously referential. All images refer to things, but it's too simple to say that the book cover merely refers to the text that it surrounds. Most book covers refer to things associated with their genre, to cultural tropes, to ideas and feelings that may have only a tenuous connection to the text. Making matters even more complicated, an image is both a thing and a representation; it is, simultaneously, an agglomeration of perceptible attributes (e.g., color, shape, and texture)

and a figuration of something else to which it bears a likeness. Indeed, even the simplest image possesses what C. S. Peirce called "firstness" and what Erwin Panofsky called "pre-iconographic qualities": the elements that we perceive instantaneously, even before we're concerned with whatever an image represents.[61]

Graphic artist Peter Curl elaborated on the idea of "firstness" in a pioneering how-to manual for jacket designers. "The attributes of any design which first engage the eye," he wrote, "are abstract ones: color, shape, line, and pattern, the *meaning* follows these." It is only after we perceive these attributes that we begin to understand them as a gestalt. "These abstract qualities," Curl continued, "are the tools of every artist and to handle them successfully he must have an instinctive feeling for harmony, balance, and rhythm."[62] So, like every image, the book cover is doubled: it is what it is (e.g., paper, ink), and it is like another thing (e.g., a snowy landscape). When dealing with a controversial manuscript, however, a book designer may want to forestall likeness or resemblance: to make a "pre-iconographic" book cover that resembles only itself. The cover for *The Incest Diary* (2017) by Anonymous, for instance, is as plain as could be, resembling (if anything) the unadorned hardback of a library remainder. Other examples come to mind. What is the right cover for *Mein Kampf*? In the era of #MeToo, how would you cover *Lolita*?

Above: Rodrigo Corral's jacket for the controversial *The Incest Diary* by Anonymous. *Right:* A first edition of Adolf Hitler's *Mein Kampf.*

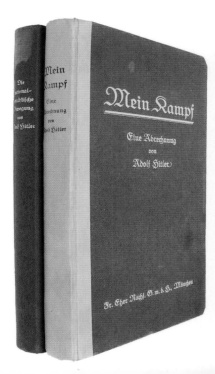

PENGUIN
BOOKS

COMPLETE   UNABRIDGED

"My first move was to do a stock take on what has already been done. Countless *Nineteen Eighty-Four* covers exist, and a good number of recent editions sit together in bookshops, so this quickly became a process concerned with what I couldn't and shouldn't do rather than what I could and should.

"I knew the idea wouldn't work if the Penguin livery wasn't in place. There would be no 'way in': nothing familiar or comforting to play against the starkness of the redaction. The book also needed to be well known to get away with this level of subversion: if potential buyers hadn't read it, there would be a good chance they would still understand the messaging. (I liked how the 'complete' and 'unabridged' line made Penguin look somehow complicit in the spread of misinformation. I have to be grateful to them for allowing such brand abuse.)

"And one last thing to mention is that Penguin understands the power of collective effect: If key content is hidden on this edition, then it can be found on another sitting close by. For a client to make this kind of leap of faith is no small thing." —David Pearson on designing George Orwell's *Nineteen Eighty-Four*.

Opposite: Nineteen Eighty-Four by George Orwell, Penguin Books, 2013, cover by David Pearson.
Right: The same book for the same publisher, designed in 1962 by Germano Facetti.

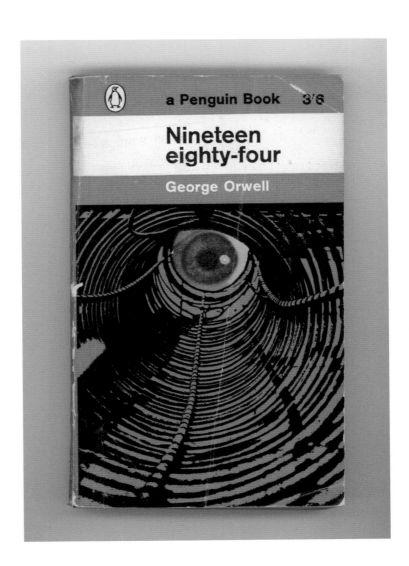

Such questions get to the heart of why the book cover matters, for they remind us that these seemingly trivial things—images that are inessential to the texts that they present to the world—can be charged with ethical and political significance, especially during turbulent times. This is partly because book design straddles the fence between art and advertising. The term "advertising" comes from the Latin *ad verte*, meaning to turn toward, and as a species of advertising, the book cover demands to be looked at. The designer is therefore responsible not only to the publisher and to the author but also to the viewing public. As image-makers, cover designers play a key role in determining how literature, both new and old, will look to the world. At its best, their job is to create images that are engaging and intelligent, perhaps also a little clever, and always sensitive to social context. They are not always successful in this regard. When Faber and Faber, for example, published a fiftieth anniversary edition of Sylvia Plath's *The Bell Jar* (2013), the cover was widely panned for badly misrepresenting the text with stereotypically feminine signifiers: bright red lips, a powder compact, manicured nails.

Instead of providing an original look for Plath's classic, this cover relies on gendered clichés in an obvious ploy to repackage *The Bell Jar* as chick lit. "Readers new to the book," wrote one journalist, "would never suspect its colossal cultural importance or that its author had stuck her head in an oven weeks before its British publication."[63] There is always a temptation toward the familiar, toward whatever worked well in the past, which can lead to the reproduction and reinforcement of misleading tropes in cover design. Examples abound: books "about Africa" that feature an acacia tree; books "about Islam" that feature a woman wearing a veil; books "about South Asia" that showcase the Taj Mahal.[64] Why do such tropes persist? In the case of the acacia tree covers, it seems that Disney's *The Lion King* (1994) has strongly influenced the way that the West visualizes the African continent. Even Chimamanda Ngozi Adichie's *Half of a Yellow Sun* (2006)—a novel that takes place during the Nigerian Civil War—has received such treatment, despite the fact that, as author and critic Jeremy Weate sardonically tweeted, "Nigeria is not known for its acacia trees." Perhaps the West is comfortable with this image because it's safe, because it presents "otherness" through a model that's easy to understand.

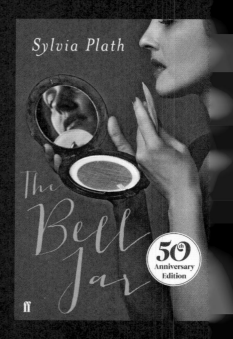

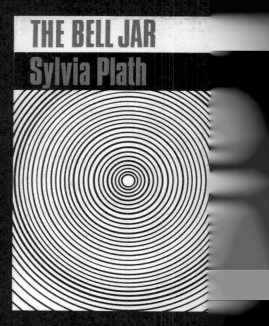

Two different covers for Sylvia Plath's *The Bell Jar*. *Top:* Faber and Faber's fiftieth anniversary edition, which was widely panned for employing gender stereotypes, packaging Plath's classic as "chick lit." *Bottom:* An earlier Faber edition whose abstract design conveys

Plath originally published *The Bell Jar*, a semi-autobiographical novel, under a pseudonym in 1963.

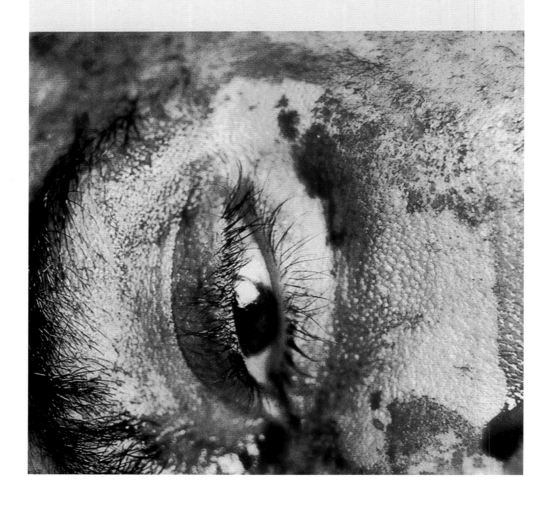

The New Testament translated by Richmond Lattimore, jacket design by Chip Kidd, photograph by Andres Serrano.

It's ironic, however, that such covers would aim to domesticate otherness. After all, reading books is one of the best ways to inhabit different, foreign, and even dangerous perspectives. Accordingly, the best covers don't try to package hard-to-swallow ideas in easily digestible form; they grapple directly with the most challenging material in the text. And in some cases, they even present *their own* challenges. Legendary cover designer Chip Kidd, for instance, sparked widespread debate when he unveiled his design for Richmond Lattimore's long-anticipated translation of the New Testament (1996). Instead of turning to a familiar piece of Christian iconography, Kidd used an Andres Serrano photograph of a cadaver in a New York City morgue. The photograph provides a close-up view of an eyeball and its surrounding skin, caked with dry blood. Striking a balance between the horrifying and the serene, the image evokes Christ's death on the cross.

But there's an added layer of complexity here. Serrano had already achieved notoriety for *Immersion (Piss Christ)* (1987)—a photograph, considered blasphemous by some, of a small crucifix submerged in the artist's urine—by the time Kidd sat down to work on the cover. Using Serrano's cadaver photograph was, therefore, a deliberate provocation. By placing a Serrano on the New Testament, Kidd implicitly argued for a reevaluation of *Piss Christ*. Perhaps, he suggested, it's not blasphemous after all; perhaps its meanings are more ambiguous and open to interpretation. At the same time, Kidd challenged people see the death of this individual, a nameless man, in relation to the death of Jesus. The cover performs a kind of resurrection: it elevates an anonymous cadaver to new life as a Christ figure, while suggesting that the loss of any life, including that of an unidentified person, deserves our attention.

A more recent, and very different, example of a challenging cover adorns Nicholson Baker's *Checkpoint* (2004). Labeled a "scummy little book" by one reviewer, *Checkpoint* tells the story of a man who wants to assassinate the then president of the United States, George W. Bush, as a way of solving the nation's problems.[65] Although *Checkpoint* is a work of fiction, it begins to sound a little *too real* as the protagonist describes his murderous intention, which is why the novel struck a nerve. Published during the height of the Iraq War, it polarized critics even before it was widely available in print. The cover, therefore, had to represent difficult, even incendiary subject matter in a highly charged political context. Outrageous designs were rejected, including one featuring Bush's head in a bull's-eye. The final cover of the first edition depicts a target with a pushpin at the center: an object described in the book, but also a metaphor that raises more questions than it answers. "Who's the pushpin?" asked reviewer Sharon Adarlo. "Who's the pinhead? Bush, the target of the assassination plot? Or the author, a pinhead for writing a book that's an easy cheap shot for anybody with a pen?"[66]

Indeed, a cover should pose some questions. Often the best design is simple, but *simple* is not the same as *simplistic*. When a cover forces you to look again, to think twice, to stop and wonder, it's respecting your intelligence, especially when it depicts sensitive subject matter. And when a cover truly wrestles with that subject matter in an original way, rather than relying on clichés, it's doing a small part to enlighten the world, inviting its viewers to think harder about received ideas and stereotypes. Isn't this the reason why books, despite all the forces arrayed against them, still remain important today? If reading is a way of changing your perspective in order to see the world through different eyes, then that process ought to begin with the look of the book.

"The Richmond Lattimore jacket was a freelance job for Little, Brown, and as such, it was pitched to me as 'How would you like to design the Bible, and make it look like a novel?' Of course, I couldn't resist, but when I suddenly arrived at the solution (I chanced upon the image in an issue of *COLORS* magazine), I knew it was right, but that it likely had no chance of getting approved. Besides being horrific, the photo was by Andres Serrano, he of the 'Piss Christ' notoriety. I submitted it anyway, because it just was the right thing to do, and I was ready to submit a kill fee when I got the call that they were going to take a chance and go with it. I was pleasantly amazed—and ultimately sorry for them, because the ensuing controversy in the press did nothing to help sales of the book. The subsequent paperback used an entirely different cover (not by me, and I don't blame them), which had a far more soothing effect and is still in print." —Chip Kidd

"This
scummy
little
book ..."

Checkpoint by Nicholson Baker,
jacket design by Peter Mendelsund.

Proposal for what was
to be printed under the
jacket for Nicholson
Baker's *Checkpoint*.

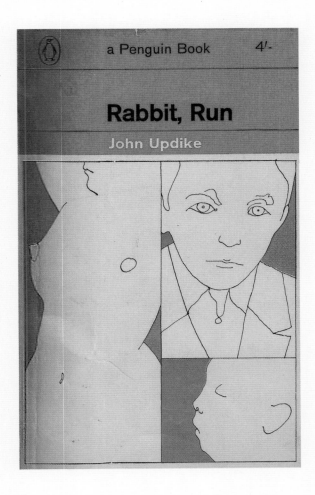

"If a book is offensive to public morals, a great cover can be its best defense. Look at Milton Glaser's cover for *Rabbit, Run* [*left*]. What does that split screen tell us? To approach Rabbit, not as a conventional hero, but like a hero of the Nouvelle Vague—haunted, self-absorbed, small in his personal relations. His lover's body is both sexual and accusing. Just because the book is concerned with sex, just because it's stylish, just because it has a male protagonist (the cover tells us), that doesn't mean it's pornographic. Or take Brownjohn, Chermayeff & Geismar's cover for *Journey to the End of the Night* [see page 227]. At first glance, an anatomical diagram; on inspection, a battle map. Suddenly we're dealing with a war novel in disguise. We have to see, not just the violence in the narrator's heart, but the violence outside him, the threat from above. Those are both fairly elaborate motifs, but look what Paul Bacon did for *Portnoy's Complaint* [see page 8] using no more than a juicy type face and a certain shade of yellow. That cover is all about the pun, the inside joke, the spirit of play—everything a censor would want you to ignore."
—Lorin Stein, editor

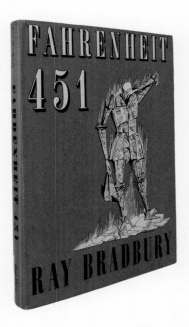

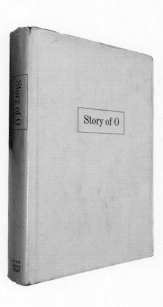

Above: Covers for controversial texts. *Fahrenheit 451* by Ray Bradbury, illustrated by Joseph Mugnaini; *The Satanic Verses* by Salman Rushdie; *Story of O* by Pauline Réage, designer uncredited.

"I've always said, my favorite thing about this cover is that anything risqué is totally in the eye of the beholder. When I show it to students, initially about a third of them can't see anything other than the corner of a room. They're the ones with sound minds. Book covers are quite small, and they're not animated, so if you can get one image to suddenly become two, you've doubled the size of your cover, and you've involved the viewer in some way—they've become coconspirators in the whole thing. And facts and figures are great, but it's even more interesting when things get confusing or ambiguous."
—Jamie Keenan, cover designer of *Lolita* by Vladimir Nabokov

Vladimir
Nabokov
Lolita

When a cover forces you to look again, to think twice, to stop and wonder, it's respecting your intelligence, especially when it depicts sensitive subject matter.

Robert Bloch

PSYCHO

"A knife on a cover these days has very little impact. It's become such a cliché of crime fiction that, for me, it holds little interest or drama. I decided to focus instead on the marks a knife would make. Those stabbing, slashing marks reminded me of water droplets, which then led me back to the famous shower scene. Using marks, tears, or cuts is a trick I use quite often. It's a great way of unifying text and image, and of pulling separate things together."
—Jonathan Gray, cover designer of *Psycho* by Robert Bloch

The cover design process for Hari Kunzru's *White Tears* (2017) is a case in point, for it raises vexing questions of identification, misidentification, appropriation, and self-awareness. Fusing the conventions of "literary" fiction with those of horror, Kunzru's novel tells the story of two white twenty-somethings who inadvertently record a Black street musician. When, at first, they try to pass off the recording as an authentic jazz song from an earlier time by a made-up recording artist, it seems like a familiar tale of "love and theft" across what W. E. B. Du Bois called "the color line," as a couple of white men, genuine admirers of jazz, seek to profit from the creativity and talent of a Black man.[67] But there's a twist: it turns out that the musician is not a product of their imagination, but an angry ghost, violently seeking retribution and reparations.

The original US jacket for *White Tears* reveals little about the content of the novel. While it includes several high-concept design details, such as concentric circles meant to mimic the look and feel of a vinyl record, its bright lettering and "big book look" don't suggest themes of racial violence. Early sketches and prototypes were much more provocative. Many feature racist caricatures: a Black male figure in a state of menacing rapture, a haunting visual representation of the specter that terrorizes the protagonists. Why is the final version tame by comparison? There isn't a simple answer to this question, since decisions of this kind are often made through multiple meetings among various stakeholders, but it's often the case that a text-based cover is used when things get too controversial. In the context of the 2016 US presidential campaign and election, which inflamed racial tensions across the nation, the more shocking prototypes came to seem insensitive rather than subversive.

While Kunzru's text invokes all these images, there's something different about representing them on a book cover, and then circulating them across the globe via digital marketing and publicity. It's one thing to see an image in your mind's eye; it's another to see it on your screen. Context matters here. For the reader of *White Tears*, themes of race and racism emerge through a complex narrative that explores cultural appropriation from multiple angles. Kunzru wants his readers to confront a history of interaction across the color line that still matters today. For the casual viewer of a book cover, however, such imagery appears (whether on the screen or in the brick-and-mortar bookstore) outside the context of the narrative. While Sambo Art might provide an accurate visualization of the text, it also carries other painful meanings that must be considered during the design process. In a digital culture of retweeting and sharing, racist imagery—even if deployed in a way that may be relevant for a certain text—has the potential to cause a lot of harm as it circulates.

The situation with the cover design of *White Tears* exemplifies a trend in contemporary fiction. In recent years, many novelists around the world have addressed race in innovative and challenging ways, which, in turn, has forced cover designers to represent texts that are both politically sensitive and ethically demanding. Yaa Gyasi, for instance, began writing *Homegoing* (2016) when she asked herself, "What does it mean to be Black in America today?"[68] Through a storytelling technique that adapts George Eliot's *Middlemarch* for our time,

This page and opposite: *White Tears* by Hari Kunzru, unused cover comps by Peter Mendelsund.

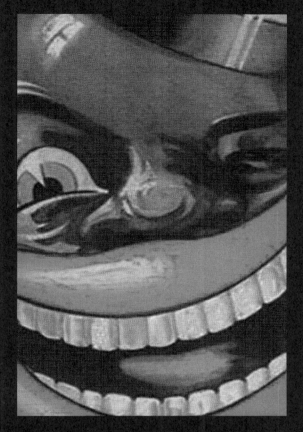

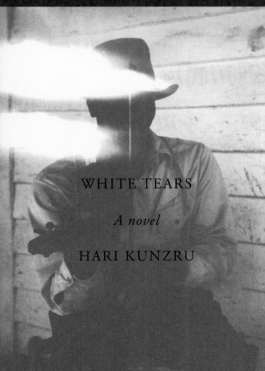

WHITE TEARS

A novel

HARI KUNZRU

WHITE TEARS
(A Novel)

Hari
KUNZRU

A NOVEL
WHITE TEARS
HARI KUNZRU

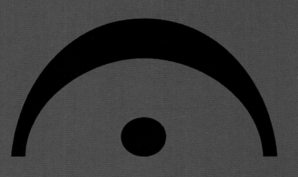

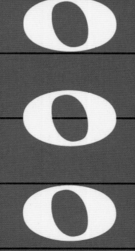

White Tears by Hari Kunzru, unused cover comps designed by Peter Mendelsund. *Opposite:* Note that the subtitle for this novel, briefly, was "A Ghost Story." Cover design can in fact influence genre assignment, rather than the other way around.

A GHOST STORY

WHITE TEARS
HARI KUNZRU

"They want the jacket to be commensurate with the expectation of the blockbuster: it has to look the part. There are things that you're not going to be able to get away with." —Oliver Munday, cover designer of *The Underground Railroad* by Colson Whitehead

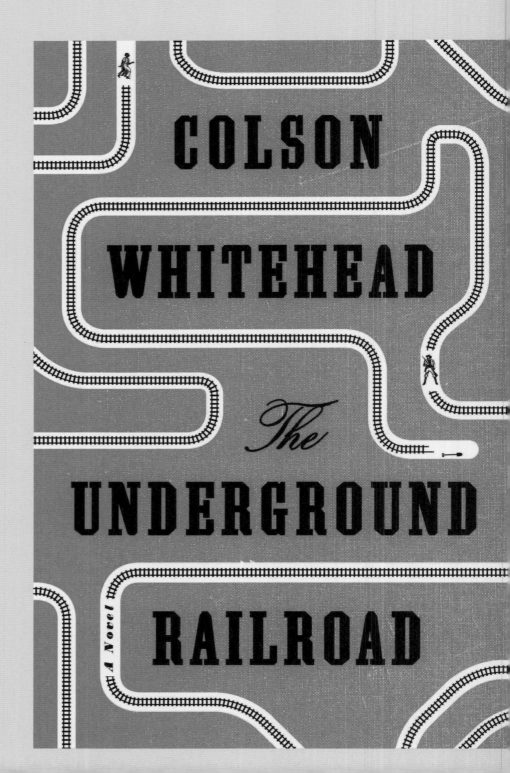

Homegoing traces three hundred years of New World slavery from Africa to America, by following the descendants of two half-sisters born in Ghana in the late eighteenth century. The protagonist of the narrative is therefore a collective one (i.e., a family) that is visualized by a genealogical diagram on the book's fourth page. As the narrative unfolds, the setting shifts from the yam fields of Ghana to the streets of Harlem, where Ralph Ellison's Invisible Man famously proclaimed, "I yam what I am." The overall pattern of the *Homegoing* jacket suggests a tapestry, and its typography calls to mind African woodcuts. The jacket also has a kind of plot, which is that of *Homegoing* itself. If you scan the image from the top left to the bottom right, "reading" the horizontal bands of visual signifiers as you would read lines of text, you can see that it tells Gyasi's whole story in an abstract spatial language that depicts burning yam fields, the Atlantic Ocean, and the skyline of New York City. The student of Modern Art will also recognize the influence of Matisse, whose paper cutouts were on display at New York's Museum of Modern Art when this cover was being designed.

Like Gyasi, Jesmyn Ward and Colson Whitehead have written powerful novels about race, and these novels have prompted similarly interesting cover designs. According to Oliver Munday, the designer for Whitehead's *The Underground Railroad* (2016), working on the jacket was rewarding but difficult, because the novel was expected to be a huge success (ultimately, it won both the Pulitzer Prize and the National Book Award). This expectation not only brought scrutiny to Munday's prototypes but also established a specific design constraint for the look of the book. "They want the jacket to be commensurate with the expectation of the blockbuster: it has to look the part," he explained. "There are things that you're not going to be able to get away with." Munday is referring specifically to the "big book look" that we discussed in chapter two. "Usually," he went on, "this means big typography: a big title-and-author-name combo that announces itself as something important and that just feels exciting and big. I don't know that anyone understands what they want when they say that; they just want to feel something."[69] Aware that he had to work with a text-heavy design, Munday created drama *around* the title and author, with railroad tracks snaking an irregular line across the jacket.

Helen Yentus, the jacket designer for Ward's *Sing, Unburied, Sing* (2017), echoed Munday's point about "feeling." Although the term "big book look" technically designates a set of formal choices and conventions, it's the feeling that matters above all. Readers of Ward's earlier fiction will know that she writes lyrically about race and poverty in the American South, and that her National Book Award–winning 2011 novel, *Salvage the Bones,* is a soaring account of post-Katrina New Orleans. Working on the jacket for *Sing, Unburied, Sing,* therefore, Yentus knew that she had to make a design that would signify "literary" without failing to attract the new readers that Ward's publisher was hoping to reach. "As a designer," she explained, "you're in a tricky place because what you're trying to do is to give art a face. You're packaging art, ideally, with what is also art, but you're working within a commercial framework."[70] For his part, Munday made this point more bluntly: "There are all these preconceived notions of what is going to put a buyer off. Even if these things aren't spoken of or made explicit, I have internalized them, so I just know." On the flip side, there are also preconceived notions about how certain books *ought* to look. Yentus's cover for *Sing, Unburied, Sing,* for instance, perfectly exemplifies the trend in high-literary publishing toward covers that employ flashy colors and dynamic interaction between text and visual figure.

For these designers, it's crucial to discern which version of the "big book look" will make the book feel, on the one hand, serious and artful and, on the other hand, inviting and accessible. While the designer always faces the commercial imperative to create an effective product package that drives sales, when dealing with literary fiction by authors such as Ward or Whitehead, the designer must grapple as well with the aesthetic demands of the manuscript. Novels like *The Underground Railroad* and *Sing, Unburied, Sing* are literary achievements, not merely publishing commodities, so their covers must reflect their artfulness. "It's always a very tricky balance," Yentus noted, "between staying true to the book, the writer, the content, and the voice, while getting the book into as many hands as you can, because that's actually your job."

Gender can influence this process. As novelist Meg Wolitzer has written, "cover illustrations are code," and too often literary novels by women are packaged as "women's fiction" through trite representations

Simon Stevens
@SimonMStevens

Like so many (wildly varying) writers on Africa, Adichie gets the acacia tree sunset treatment...
(@AfricasaCountry)

"Nigeria is not known for its acacia trees."

of femininity that undermine the aesthetic sophistication of the text. "Certain images," Wolitzer writes, "are geared toward women as strongly as an ad for 'calcium plus D.' These covers might as well have a hex sign slapped on them, along with the words: 'Stay away, men! Go read Cormac McCarthy instead!'" Every book buyer has seen what Wolitzer is referring to; just think of the many recent covers and jackets that depict a long-haired young girl in a flowing dress, her face turned coyly away from the camera. Male authors, by contrast, are more likely to receive designs that feature large author-and-title combinations, which suggest the arrival of literary greatness. "If *The Marriage Plot*, by Jeffrey Eugenides," Wolitzer asks, "had been written by a woman yet still had the same title and wedding ring on its cover, would it have received a great deal of serious literary attention?"[71]

This question invites us to consider the "code" of the book cover: the unspoken assumptions that determine the look of the book. Just as there are clichés associated with specific literary genres—the alcoholic private eye, the priest who's lost his faith, the damsel in distress—so too are there hackneyed visual conceits for representing a new novel and for positioning it in the marketplace. Whether online or in the bookstore, a new book needs first and foremost to catch a browser's eye, and in order to do so, the cover must stand out in some way. Many covers in a given season, however, tend to imitate each other. Instead of looking original, they look like what came before, or worse, they look like whatever their genre is *supposed to look like*. In many cases, publishers want covers that they think are safe bets, which is to say covers that resemble

Book covers fail whenever they rely on problematic stereotypes to represent the subject matter of the text. *Above:* Books "about Africa" whose covers employ a visual cliché, the acacia tree, for how Africa looks through Western eyes.

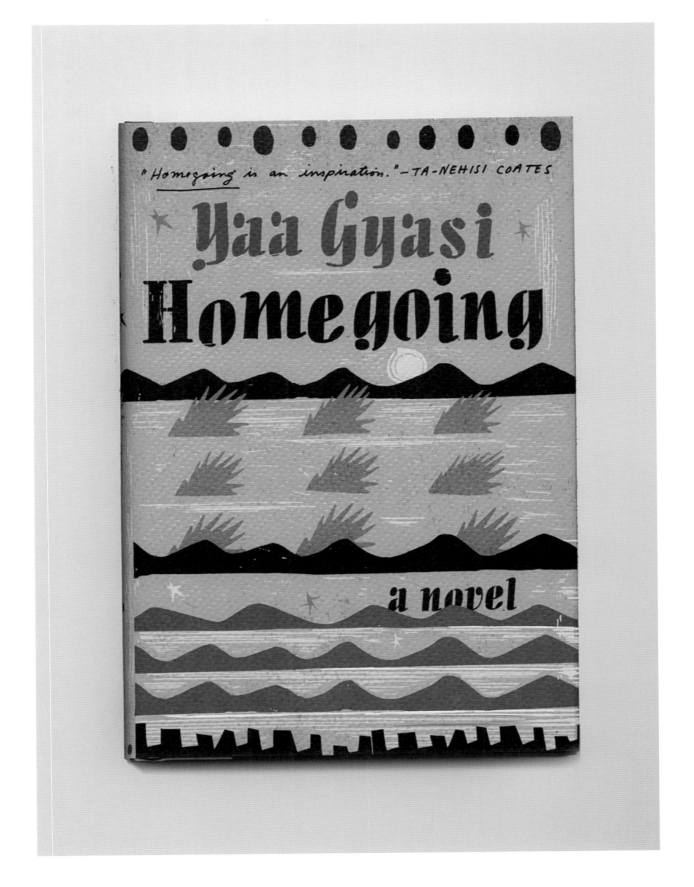

Homegoing by Yaa Gyasi, Alfred A. Knopf, cover design by Peter Mendelsund. Scan the image from the top left to the bottom right, "reading" the horizontal bands of visual signifiers as you would read lines of text.

rld of
rie
ng

T

Men
of a
Geisha

a novel by

A MAJOR MOTION PICT

NORWEGIA

THE
MAKIOKA SISTERS

JUNICHIRŌ
TANIZAKI

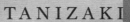
"A masterpiece of great beauty
and quality." —*Chicago Tribune*

YOU

RUKI
AKAMI

those that have worked in the past. Unfortunately, by dictating that designers produce genre-ready, copycat covers, publishers are ensuring that their books will get lost amid the clones.

Such covers might misrepresent the author's text, as in the case of Faber and Faber's *The Bell Jar* (see page 190). A more complicated example is the US paperback covers of Italian novelist Elena Ferrante's Neapolitan tetralogy (see page 210). Ferrante's critically acclaimed novels tell the story of friendship between two women over fifty years. They're distinctive literary achievements that have won Ferrante a passionate readership outside her native Italy, while earning her work a rightful place in the emerging canon of twenty-first-century fiction. Their covers, however, downplay their literariness, making them resemble what one reviewer has called the "$4 romance book found in an American gas station."[72] According to the art director, this choice was intentional, if also controversial: "Many people didn't understand the game we're playing," she rued, "that of, let's say, dressing an extremely refined story with a touch of vulgarity."[73]

But these covers do more than force a juxtaposition of "high" and "low" culture, refined and profane aesthetics. They also raise the question of how gender intersects with taste. In a convincing defense of Ferrante's covers, Emily Harnett argued that "to despise the covers—and, by extension, the kind of novel they evoke—in the name of *good* literature is to buy into the destructive stigma that has long been attached to 'women's fiction' as a genre."[74] Her point is that it's fine to dislike the covers because you find them dull or trite, but as soon as you see them as sullying the "high" art of Ferrante's writing with the "low" trappings of women's fiction, you're firming up a false dichotomy and perpetuating the sexist notion that women's fiction can't be "serious" literature. Rebecca Solnit succinctly described this dichotomy when she wrote, "a book without women is often said to be about humanity, but a book with women in the foreground is a woman's book."[75]

Perhaps, however, the problems of sexism and gender bias reside precisely in the concept of "humanity"—that is, in whatever "the human" is understood to be—which makes them crucial problems for design. Caroline Criado Perez, author of *Invisible Women:*

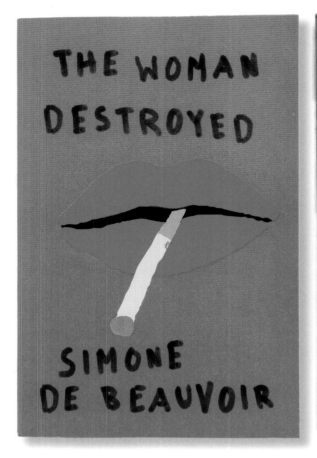
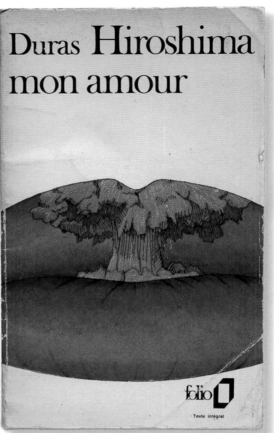

Some book covers blatantly reinforce clichés of gender (see pages 206 and 207). Others engage with familiar tropes, figures, and conventions in order to create something new. *Above left: The Woman Destroyed* by Simone de Beauvoir, cover by Peter Mendelsund. *Above right: Hiroshima mon amour* by Marguerite Duras, 1981, illustration by Frédéric Blaimont.

Exposing Data Bias in a World Designed for Men (2019), has pointed out that the "default" notion of the generic human is, in fact, not generic at all. Unless otherwise defined by gender, the human (or "the user") means cisgendered man. "Seeing men as the human default," she writes, "is fundamental to the structure of human society. It's an old habit and it runs deep—as deep as theories of human evolution itself."[76] Indeed, Perez was stunned when she became conscious of this habit in her own mind: "Whenever I pictured anyone, and the gender wasn't specified, I was picturing a man: a lawyer, a doctor, a journalist, a scientist, anyone, I was constantly picturing men. And that was really shocking to me—not only the fact that I was doing that, but the fact that I hadn't noticed that I was doing that."[77]

Of course, books are not all that is needed to fix the problem of the "default male," which permeates culture, society, and design. What books can do is challenge our habits and make us more aware of the biases that structure our thinking. For an author such as Ferrante, this means inviting readers to think about women, not in the abstract, but as historical actors, living in a specific time and place. The richly defined *particularity* of Ferrante's characters—their psychological profiles, their moods and emotions, their ways of navigating relationships—is what makes them emblematic of "the human." And representing women in this way, avoiding the clichés of gender

THE BURNING GIRL

GIRL

CLAIRE MESSUD

A NOVEL

The Burning Girl by Claire Messud, chosen cover comp designed by Peter Mendelsund. How can the cliché of female hands on covers be deployed in a way that evokes something new?

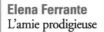

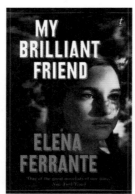
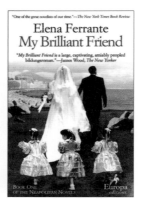

Some of the many different covers for Elena Ferrante's Neapolitan Novels. A global sensation, Ferrante's novels have been translated and published in different markets, which demand different cover designs and marketing strategies.

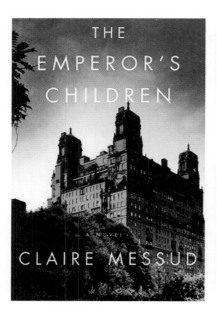
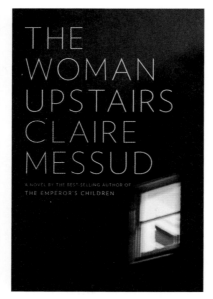

Cover designs by Carol Devine Carson for Alfred A. Knopf.

in favor of more nuanced and diverse characterizations, presents the best kind of challenge for the cover designer, who must strive to do justice to the author's vision.

Consider, as a final example, Claire Messud's *The Woman Upstairs* (2013), which opens with a screed by the narrator, Nora. "How angry am I?" Nora asks. "You don't want to know. Nobody wants to know about *that*," but she tells us anyway:

> *I'm a good girl, I'm a nice girl, I'm a straight-A, strait-laced, good daughter, good career girl, and I never stole anybody's boyfriend and I never ran out on a girlfriend, and I put up with my parents' shit and my brother's shit, and I'm not a girl anyhow, I'm over forty fucking years old, and I'm good at my job and I'm great with kids and I held my mother's hand when she died, after four years of holding her hand while she was dying, and I speak to my father every day on the telephone—every day, mind you, and what kind of weather do you have on your side of the river, because here it's pretty gray and a bit muggy too? It was supposed to say "Great Artist" on my tombstone, but if I died right now it would say "such a good teacher/daughter/friend" instead; and what I really want to shout, and want in big letters on that grave, too, is FUCK YOU ALL.*[78]

Imagine you're the book designer. How might you visualize this text? It's a difficult question because covers are supposed to be attractive and inviting, but Messud's narrator is intentionally unlikable.[79] While working on the cover for Messud's earlier novel, *The Emperor's Children* (2006), designer Carol Devine Carson reports that she was struck by the "sensual and visual" qualities of the narrative.

"There was architecture, food, weather, scents, and definitely, the place, New York City," Carson explains. "I recalled an image from a photographer's book—Jan Staller—clearly of the Upper West Side. This cemented the locale, possibly The Beresford, near Central Park, so important to the story. I hoped it would give Messud's readers an idea and picture of her families' lives."[80]

As its title suggests, *The Woman Upstairs* also includes vivid representations of place and space, but its narration poses a distinct challenge for the designer. As we have been suggesting throughout this book, covers are connectors that bring disparate people together, but Nora wants no connection whatsoever. She is angry and alienating. The designer of a novel like this one must confront the tension between accurately representing the text and piquing the interest of a potential reader. What does "fuck you all" look like on a book cover? How do you represent an insult without being insulting?

It's yet another interesting question raised by the process of cover design. And perhaps, above all, it's the *questioning* prompted by the book cover that makes the book cover matter. On the one hand, covers are merely images; they adorn and frame the text that is assumed to be the *actual* work of art. On the other hand, it's precisely because they are images that book covers prompt questions, invite speculations, demand critique, and, occasionally, change your perspective on the world. The cover resides at the intersection of art, culture, commerce, and design, which is why thinking about it involves thinking about so much else. And now that we've considered why the book cover matters and, hopefully, convinced you that it does, we are prepared to look behind the curtain at how the book cover gets made. As we'll see in the next chapter, the mechanics of cover design prompt questions all their own.

What does "fuck you all" look like on a book cover? How do you represent an insult without being insulting?

"I'm raging! Fuming! Panting! With hatred! Hypocrites!"
—Louis-Ferdinand Céline's preface to the 1952 Gallimard edition of *Journey to the End of the Night*.

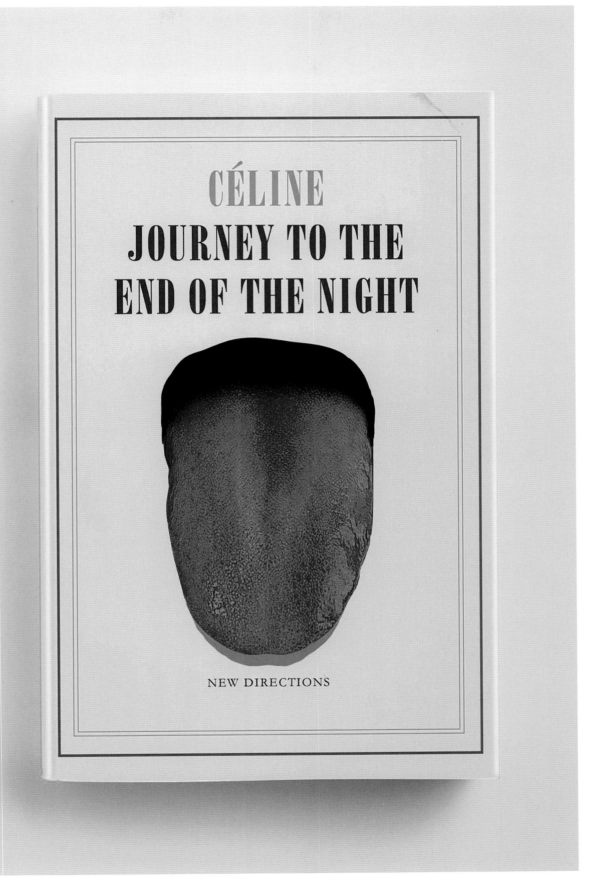

Roald Dahl

Switch Bitch

Confessions of the Flesh
The History of Sexuality,
Volume 4 **Michel Foucault**

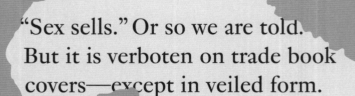

"Sex sells." Or so we are told.
But it is verboten on trade book
covers—except in veiled form.

'Uninhibited, erotic, delicious...'
JOHN UPDIKE

Fear of Flying

ERICA JONG

Opposite left: *Switch Bitch* by Roald Dahl, Penguin Books, 1981, cover by David Pelham. *Opposite right:* How to shoehorn sin, sex, and eleventh- to fourteenth-century Christianity into the same jacket. *The History of Sexuality, Volume 4*, by Michel Foucault, design by Peter Mendelsund. *This page: Fear of Flying* by Erica Jong, jacket design by Julia Connolly.

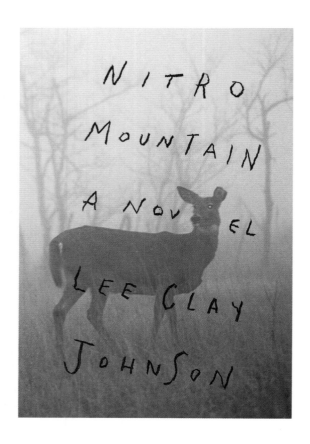

"'Intimate; don't show,' might be a good principle for designing jackets for books with violent content. It follows from the premise in film that fear builds in the anticipation, rather than in the thing itself. Bearing this in mind, I avoided any attempt to render the menacing, maniacal character at the center of *Nitro Mountain*. Instead, I imagined the typography as written by his unstable hand. Behind the words is a moody photo of the Shenandoah Valley (where the book is partially set); a deer alerted to footsteps."

—Oliver Munday, cover designer of *Nitro Mountain* by Lee Clay Johnson

"It always bothered me that on the original cover of *American Psycho*, Patrick Bateman's face was so clearly defined. That's something I've always strenuously avoided—literally depicting a fictitious character. It could rob the reader of the unique experience of deciding for themselves what the characters look like. Reading prose is a theater of the mind, and I don't want to over-direct it. Anyway, my cover for *AP* lets you fill in the blanks. It suggests what you might see if someone slipped something into your drink, and that someone is there right in front of you, and, well, it's starting to take effect. And in a few moments, you might not see anything else, ever again … "

—Chip Kidd, cover designer of *American Psycho* by Bret Easton Ellis

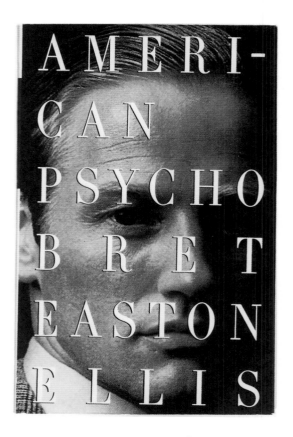

How the
Book Cover
Is Made

5.

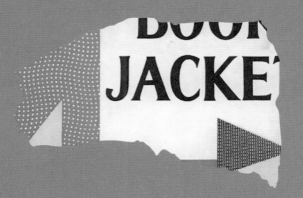
BOOK
JACKET

"When presenting my design department's average weekly output of twenty to thirty prospective cover concepts to a hardheaded and rather formidable board of editorial directors and marketing people, I would occasionally present a carefully designed decoy turkey that I would pretend to fiercely defend. Upon its unanimous rejection, I would 'reluctantly' accept defeat and go with an also-ran, which, of course, was the design of my choice and would be accepted with obvious relief by the board. Over time, however, they caught on to my tactics, and second-guessing worthy of Spassky and Fisher would ensue. So there's a lot more to an art director's role than just waving a pencil around in the manner of a conductor's baton."
—David Pelham, designer

"I always tell myself: 'You're not the star of the show. The author took three and a half years to write the goddamn thing, and the publisher is spending a fortune on it, so just back off.'"
—Paul Bacon, designer

Charles Rosner had some advice for young designers. As chief curator of the first international museum exhibition of book jackets, held at the Victoria and Albert Museum in 1949, he was an authority on the topic. "The artist will read the script," Rosner wrote, "not only projecting himself into its atmosphere, but drawing from it the essential quality of the author's creation; then, and only then, will he begin to consider how best he can interpret it in his own medium so that his final design will truly represent the distinctive flavour and factual content of the book itself."[81] Times have changed, but this advice still holds. Good cover design begins with deeply immersive reading. And the best covers render something more than a figure, a composition, or a collage of image and text. They disclose how it *feels* to inhabit the author's world.

Rosner was on to something. He considered deeply immersive reading to be the first step in the design process, precisely because "in the arts," as Henry James once wrote, "feeling is always meaning."[82] This claim is especially apt for cover art, since the book cover must calibrate feeling and meaning in subtle ways. Book covers simultaneously show and tell; they provide both information and sensation. The key facts about the book at hand (title, author, publisher, genre) are delivered through an overall design, whose color, shape, and texture set the mood. In this sense, the cover functions as a sort of barometer, indexed to the internal weather, the "atmosphere" as it were, inside the book. Designers often play with this relationship. On the one hand, many of the most successful covers create some friction between inside and outside, between the look of the book and the feeling of the text. On the other hand, many of the biggest flops in cover art push too far in their own direction, to the point that they fail to represent what Rosner calls the "essential quality of the author's creation."

Making a successful book cover, in other words, requires some restraint. The designer must strike a delicate balance between word and image, author's vision and designer's skill, through a process of reverse *ekphrasis*. Dating all the way back to ancient Greece, *ekphrasis* designates "the verbal representation of visual representation," or the literary description of a visual object, such as the shield of Achilles in Homer's *Iliad*.[83] Today's cover designers invert this process: they give visual form to the images and atmospheres of verbal art.

So, how is a book cover made? And what makes a successful book cover? The fundamental techniques of cover design are not all that difficult to learn. The formula is pretty straightforward: read, think, sketch, iterate, pitch, solicit feedback, revise, pitch again, and eventually get approval. Achieving the desired result is another matter. Like any serious creative endeavor, cover design takes practice and patience, a point emphasized by Peter Curl in an early instruction manual for aspiring cover designers. Published in 1956, a few years after Rosner's exhibition, Curl's *Designing a Book Jacket* remains among the most incisive treatments of the topic.[84] To be sure, some of his advice now sounds dated—a chapter on "Equipment and Materials" mentions compasses, pencils, and T squares, rather than MacBooks and Adobe—but the fundamentals of cover design are not so different today than they were in the middle of the twentieth century. Indeed, *Designing a Book Jacket* just needs a little updating for the digital age.

If the 1949 exhibition was a sign that, as Curl puts it, "the book jacket ha[d] achieved the standing of a serious activity for the graphic artist," then his book was a first step toward consolidating this activity as a bona fide art form, making it respectable by differentiating it from mere advertising.[85] The book jacket may be a product package, Curl argued, but it is "selling something infinitely more subtle and complicated than soapflakes."[86] He was writing at the height of the pulp paperback era in the United States and England, when delightfully garish book covers were glutting the market with sensational images of scantily clad women and scenes of lurid violence. While we may look back on these covers with some nostalgia today, they posed a threat to the designer seeking to elevate his craft above the schlock of the pulps.[87] "There is one type of jacket that will not be considered at all," Curl writes in his introduction. "This is the jacket which exploits sadism or sex by portraying anatomically exaggerated ladies inadequately draped. If a book jacket design is to maintain its dignity as a branch of graphic art it must have no dealings with this debased style."[88]

To be sure, Curl sounds a little prudish, but as discussed in the previous chapter, designers face many of the same challenges today. Even if sex sells, cover designers must avoid sexism. In a world where the basic mandate of every book cover is to instantly capture attention while standing out from the competition, there is always a temptation to be as provocative as possible. Still, there is no denying the new commercial and cultural realities of online retailing and social media. If you're seeking a new book in today's retail environment, it's likely that your search will begin with Google and end with Amazon, where half of all book purchases in the United States are made.[89] Social media play an increasingly prominent role in spreading the word about a new title, while authors (and designers) self-market their wares on Instagram and elsewhere. At the same time, though, the independent bookstore has made a comeback. Overwhelmed by the flood of choices, and fatigued by algorithmically generated recommendations, consumers crave this expertly curated boutique experience.

What's a cover designer to do in this context? It seems an impossible situation: on the one hand, the cover must look great as a tiny digital thumbnail; on the other hand, it must provide a satisfying experience as a physical, tangible thing. And as if reconciling these imperatives were not difficult enough, the best covers do even more—they're honest, clever *enhancements* of the author's text that enrich the overall aesthetic experience of the book. The stakes are high: one prominent literary agent, Chris Parris-Lamb, believes that cover design is "the single most important factor" in determining whether a book will be a success in today's retail climate.[90] Moreover, as journalist Margot Boyer-Dry has noted in her reporting on this topic, even though sales of print books have increased by 11 percent since 2013, revenues have decreased in the era of online shopping. "This leaves publishers with a killer combination of higher stakes and fewer resources," Boyer-Dry writes, "which leads in turn to safer choices."[91]

Perhaps Curl's *Designing a Book Jacket* can offer some advice. This how-to manual remains an important resource for the cover designer. Curl's premise is that, in order "to give graphic form" to any manuscript, the cover designer "must be an artist and a craftsman and have a feeling for books."[92] Talent and technical skill are not enough, he suggests; the designer must possess an intuitive connection to the affect and atmosphere created by the written word. In the simplest sense, this means *reading* the manuscript, getting lost for a time in the world that the author has created, daydreaming by the book. Curl cautions the designer, however, to avoid taking "too literally" the publisher who exclaims, "Do just what you like," for the end product is never "entirely up to you!"[93] Indeed, this is always a trap. Good design emerges though a collaborative process. While some elements of this process (e.g., ideation, sketching) may occur in private, the end product is never the designer's alone. Making a successful book cover requires asking questions, soliciting input, and working with a team of professionals, some of whom are neither designers nor passionate readers, but experts nonetheless. The idea of the isolated genius, toiling away in seclusion and then emerging triumphant, has no place here.

In addition to works of art and design, book covers are, in a sense, data visualizations. As Curl explains, they "must display certain information; the title, the author's name, and the name of the publisher must appear whether the design is treated in an abstract, symbolic, or pictorial manner." However, "there can be infinite variety in the arrangement and treatment of the obligatory elements in the design."[94] All design begins with a *constraint*: in other words, and in the case of the book cover, the designer enters the process knowing that particular pieces of information must be displayed on the finished product. In addition, the designer must grapple with norms, conventions, and unspoken rules regarding the look of the book—above all, the notion that a certain book *should look* a certain way in order to provide the right visual cues. The best design treats all this as a productive challenge, rather than merely an annoying limitation.

The idea of *constraint* in book design is also spatial—it can be understood in terms of real estate, geography, and figure-ground relations—since only so much room is available on any cover. Curl notes that the "spine presents a special problem to the designer."[95] If you remove a book jacket from a hardcover and place it flat on a table, you'll see that it has five rectangular spaces for design and illustration, the narrowest being the one covering the book's spine. For the designer, this piece of real estate is both exclusive and cramped (think: studio apartment in the best neighborhood of a dense city). To make this space work, the designer must be shrewd, not only because the space is small but also because it will function as the outward face of the book for much of the book's life. In addition to conveying essential information—author, title, publisher—the spine may carry an illustration from the front or back flap. In any case, the goal is to integrate the spine panel with the other parts of the jacket, while giving this narrow strip enough flair to make it stand out from other books on the shelf.

One way to achieve a memorable-looking book is through lettering. Curl goes so far as to argue that "every designer should be able to carry out the lettering on his jackets," because "letters alone, well designed and well arranged, can produce the most distinctive decorative design."[96] Of course, letters are not only constituent parts of words that communicate meanings; they are also shapes, patterns, and arrangements. At the outset of any project, the designer will want to make broad decisions, including the decision of whether lettering or art/illustration will be the main figure on the front cover. In other words, will the cover emphasize typography or calligraphy, or will it emphasize a visual image that the lettering must accommodate? If type is the star of the show, then the designer has many options for how to manipulate letters and words *as shapes*. But if the cover will feature a visual image, then the central question regarding typography is serif or sans serif? Much has been written about the difference between these two options, and the general consensus seems to be that serif typefaces suggest *classical* values while sans serif typefaces suggest *modern* ones.[97] The talented designer will experiment with, and perhaps challenge, this dichotomy. However, it's important to remember that the lettering on the cover is meant for display as part of an overall aesthetic composition, which differentiates it from body copy, the text *inside* the book.

Curl makes two final claims that are especially resonant today. First, he contends that "each book should be considered as a unique opportunity for graphic interpretation."[98] Even if a particular book cover is not especially artful, it is nevertheless an interpretation of the text at hand. Through visual and tactile signifiers, the cover provides a context for the author's writing; it makes you see the book in a particular way. That said, design often operates beneath the threshold of conscious perception, influencing you without your knowledge, at least at first. Good design just "works" and doesn't demand critical scrutiny for doing so. But truly great design both works and stands up to scrutiny. Perhaps this is why the best book covers change with you as you read.

And second, Curl writes, "A good book jacket is an honest book jacket."[99] What might "honest" mean in this context? Perhaps it means that the book cover is a genuine response to the text, or that the design lands in the sweet spot between commercial imperatives and artistic expression, or that the cover is a clever interpretation of the writer's narrative, or all of the above. Perhaps "honest" also means truthful, accurate, and fair, since nothing can ruin a good book jacket like false advertising. At the same time,

"Probably the best-known design I ever made." —Ernst Reichl. Dummy for the first American edition of *Ulysses*.

6246

NIGHTWOOD DJUNA BARNES

NC

NIGHTWOOD

LINE
AS IT
COMES

Peinture
in blue

LINE
AS IT
COMES

lustig

remove guidelines   same size

1928

"honest" might mean persuasive (as in: "You'll like it when we get there, honest!"), or hard earned (as in: "She makes an honest living."), or morally correct, sincere, and blameless. It suffices to say that an honest book jacket fulfills its mandate, which is to broker a delicate relationship between the text and the world, to invite us "in" to the book while making the book presentable, ready for the limelight.

"If I seem to place a heavy mantle of responsibility on the shoulders of those who are really only expected to make nice shapes and colors, it is because history demands it."
—Alvin Lustig, designer

With these principles in mind, we can now turn to the question of *process*. What, exactly, does the cover designer do? How is the book cover made, step-by-step? While every cover designer or design team will have their own working methods and practices, and while every new commission will present its own challenges and opportunities, the cover-design process generally involves the following steps: reading the manuscript, reflecting on the project, asking big-picture design questions, choosing appropriate subject matter, sketching by hand, designing digitally, iterating, pitching, revising, and ultimately winning approval.

Reading and thinking come first. Instead of relying on a summary of the book's contents, the designer will want to read the manuscript, in order to search for visual signifiers that might serve as emblems for the book as a whole. In a way, the designer is the book's first critic. Before the book ever receives a much-hoped-for review in the *New Yorker* or a reaction on Twitter, the designer is already assessing, interpreting, and considering how to "frame" the work at hand. Thus, the designer will want to ask big questions while reading: What medium of expression (e.g., photography, illustration, pencil, pen, paint, vector, etc.) works for this commission? Who makes up the intended audience, and how can they be reached? What broad design category (e.g., abstract, representational, collage) will serve the text? Calligraphy or typography? Serif or sans serif? Color palette? More than anything else, these broad choices

Nightwood by Djuna Barnes, design by Alvin Lustig, 1947. *Opposite:* The original mechanical.

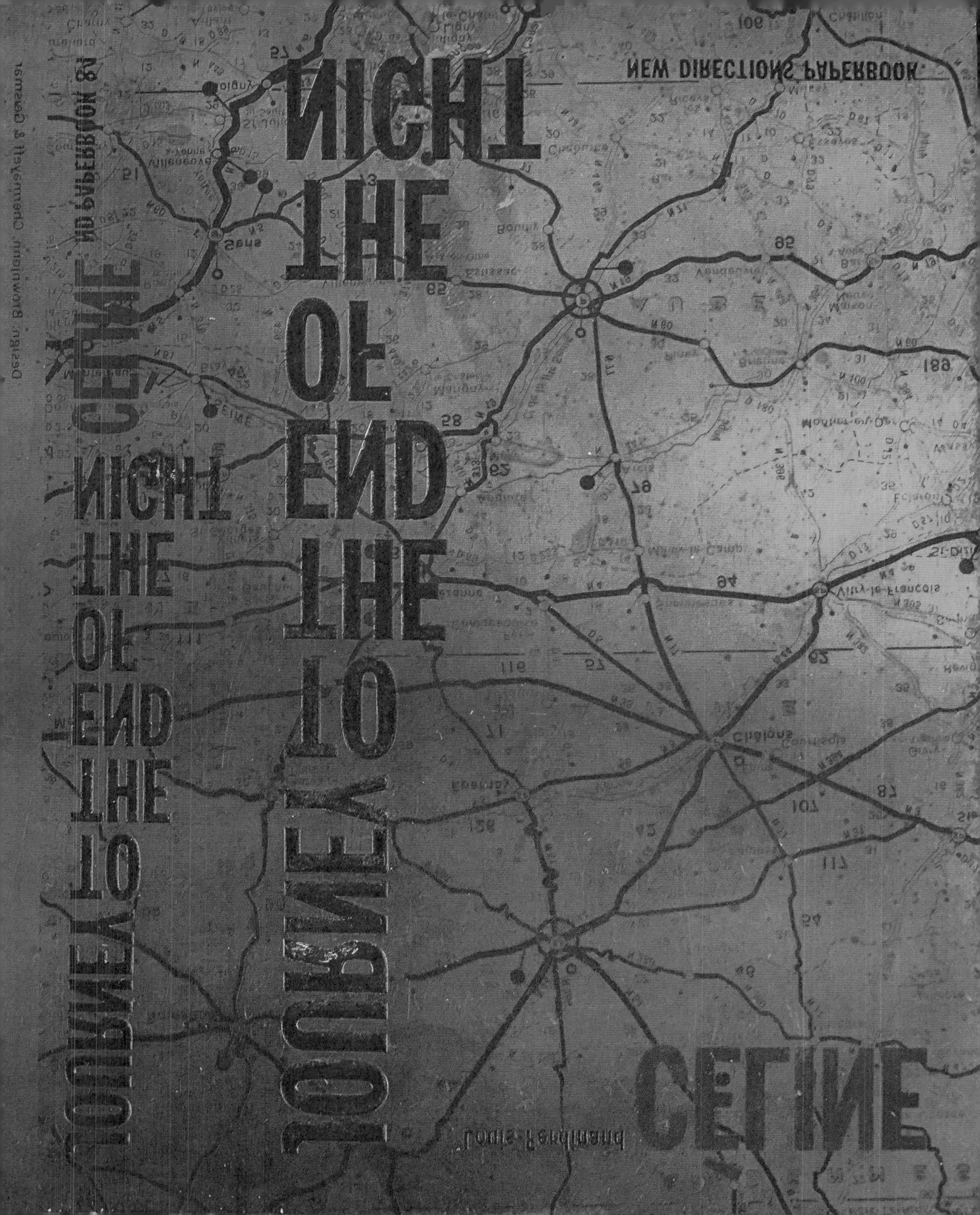

NIGHT
THE
OF
END
THE

JOURNEY TO

CÉLINE

Design: Brownjohn, Chermayeff & Geismar

"At first glance, an anatomical diagram; on inspection, a battle map." —Lorin Stein, editor

Opposite: Printing plate for the cover of *Journey to the End of the Night* (*this page*) by Louis-Ferdinand Céline, 1960, designed by Brownjohn, Chermayeff & Geismar.

will determine the mood of the cover: the all-important, instantaneous, and almost subliminal *feeling* that the book gives off to a potential buyer or reader.

Next, it's time to choose appropriate subject matter for the cover. Putting a human figure on the cover can be a winning strategy, but it's also a risky one, for this approach can "give away" too much and lead to a design that not only competes with the text but also impedes the reader's freedom to imagine. This is because *what we see when we read* is closely related to *what authors don't say when they write*. Consider, for example, the case of *Moby-Dick*. What does Melville's narrator, Ishmael, look like? Does Melville ever *describe* his physical appearance? Certainly not in the way that he describes the physicality of other memorable characters aboard the *Pequod*. And yet, as readers of the novel, we *feel* that we can picture Ishmael: he is ours. The opening pages of *Moby-Dick* put us on intimate terms with their narrator, but Melville animates Ishmael without fully describing him. Instead, we are left to fill in the gaps, which is one reason why film adaptations of books can feel like violations.

An alternative approach is to avoid human representation altogether. Material objects are saturated with metaphorical meanings—they tell us a lot about the atmosphere, tone, and place of the book, even as they disclose information about character and theme—which is why they often make good cover images. Representing an event, a place, or a time period on the cover can be a good choice, as well. This choice is especially effective for both historical and "genre" fiction, in which the setting of the narrative is highly significant to both plot and character development. On the other hand, some books are best served by a text-based cover. This can be true of celebrity authors (whose names alone can sell the book) as well as controversial manuscripts (whose contents are difficult to render visually). In any case, the manifold job of any cover is to be accurate, enticing, artful, and perhaps a little clever. Keeping these aims in mind, the cover designer will sketch, design, iterate, pitch, and revise until receiving final approval.

In the end, designing a book cover is a process of remediation and distillation. The cover designer, as both Curl and Rosner pointed out years ago, converts a long and often complex piece of written work into a single image that can be consumed in an instant. For this reason, a cover can seem like a reduction or perversion of meaning—less than the author intended, inadequate to the manuscript that it supposedly represents. At its best, though, cover design is a generous act, for it plays a major role, perhaps the most important role, in connecting authors with readers, even as it carves out a space for the written word in a predominantly visual culture. In this sense, a good book cover is not only an enticing piece of marketing; it's a small act of faith in the value of long-form writing in a culture of hot takes.

What is the future of the book cover? No one has a definitive answer to this question. We're living through a media revolution whose end point is unclear. Nonetheless, in the next chapter we risk a few speculations, based on our own experiences and on conversations with publishing professionals, technology executives, writers, and designers. What we do know is that the book cover attained its current status as a distinct medium of graphic art during the earlier media revolution called Modernism, so it's likely to continue evolving in the future.

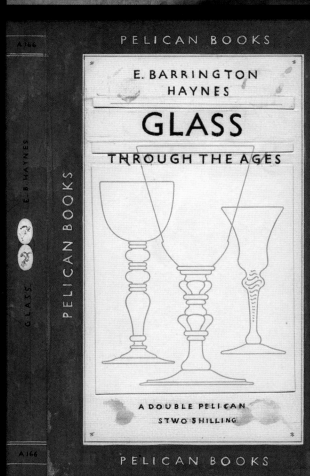

Top left:
David Pelham's sketch for *The Terminal Beach* by J. G. Ballard. "This was long before mobile phones, computers, and email. Everything had to be pasted by hand, drawn in ink on separate transparent overlays, and then collected and delivered by messengers."

Top right: Jonathan Gray's hand-painted typography for *Everything Is Illuminated* by Jonathan Safran Foer, a jacket that brought back the use of painted and handwritten type on covers.

Bottom: An experimental layout by Jan Tschichold and Erik Ellegaard Frederiksen for Pelican Books.

Francis Cugat's drafts
and final gouache painting
for the book jacket of
the first edition of *The
Great Gatsby* by F. Scott
Fitzgerald.

The decline of Postmodernism and the rise of digital technology ... have defined cover art in our time. *Below:* The contemporary design workspace.

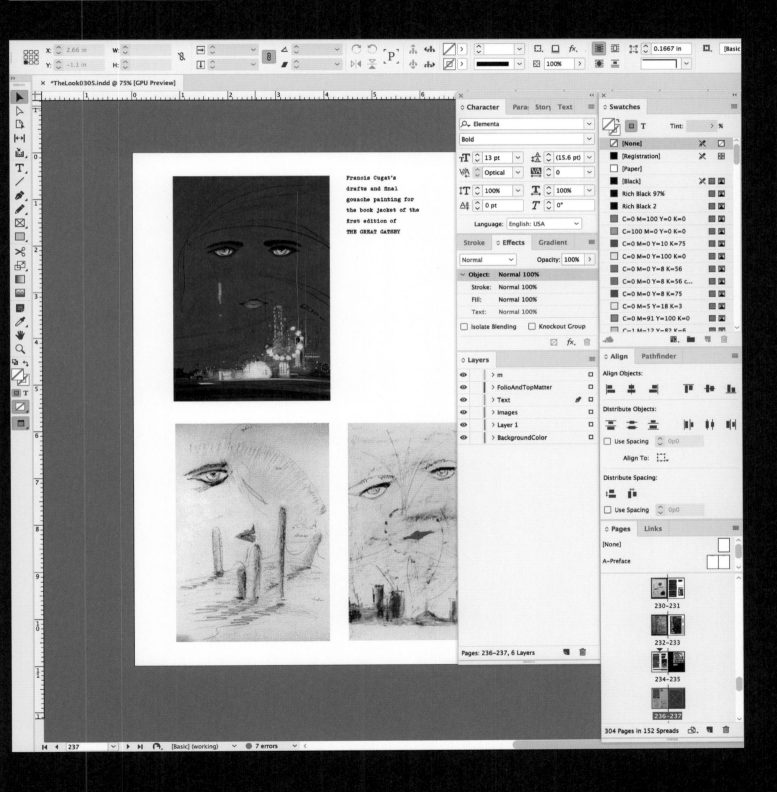

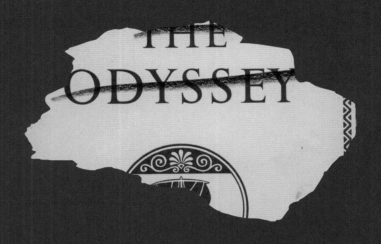

6.

Two Case Studies:
Ulysses and *Moby-Dick*

Ulysses explorations by Peter Mendelsund: overwriting.

ULYSSES

~~HOMER~~

~~THE~~

~~ODYSSEY~~

James

TR~~ANSLATED~~

~~E. V. RIEU~~

~~THE PENGUIN~~

85c

Joyce

Ulysses explorations by Peter Mendelsund: important
themes—vision and sight, the female backside.

ames

oyce

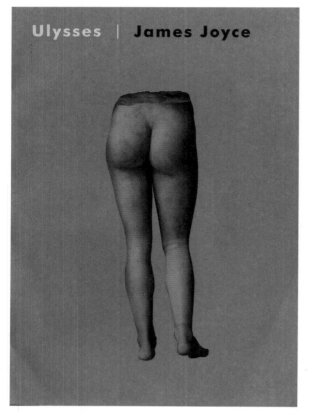

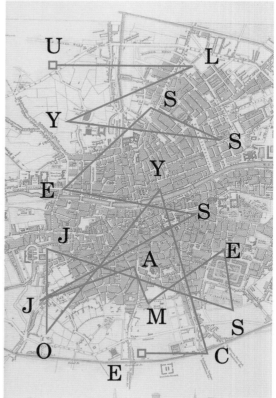

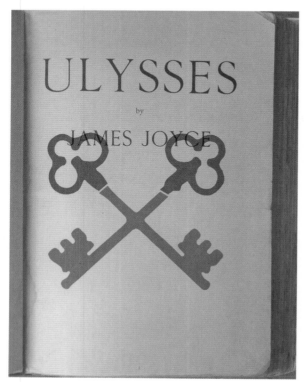

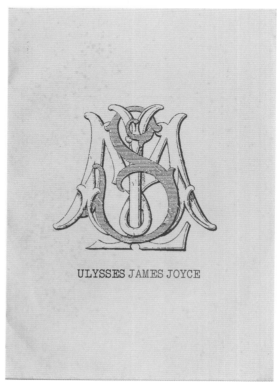

Ulysses explorations by Peter Mendelsund: *(clockwise from top left)*: Bloom's statue; wandering rocks; the holy trinity of Steven, Molly, and Leo; the crossed keys.

James Joyce's ULYSSES

Ulysses exploration by Peter Mendelsund: the mysterious
"man in the Mackintosh"—the author himself?

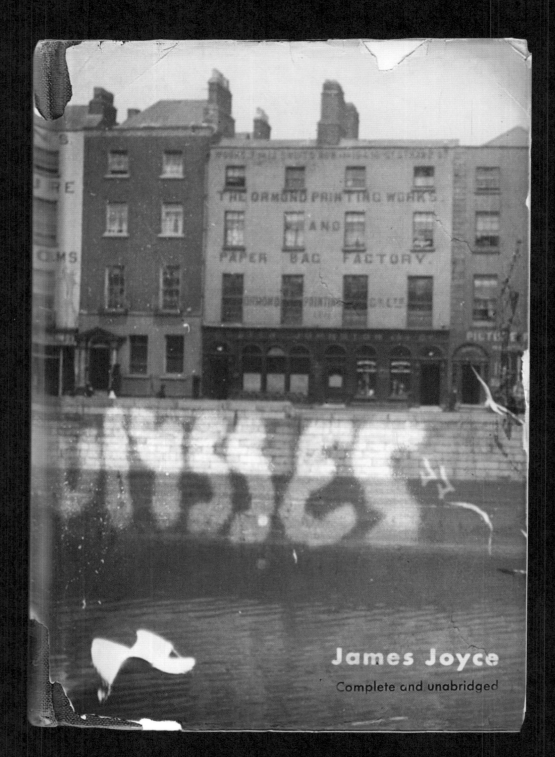

Ulysses explorations by Peter Mendelsund: the vernaculars of the quay, and of the street.

James Joyce

Complete and unabridged

"Call me
Ishmael

Moby Dick

A Novel

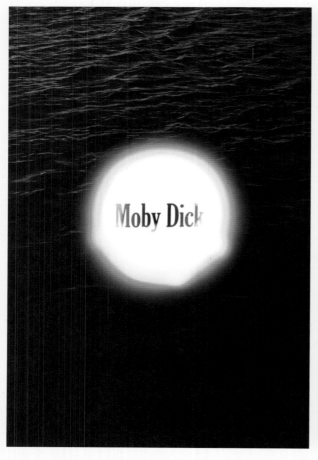
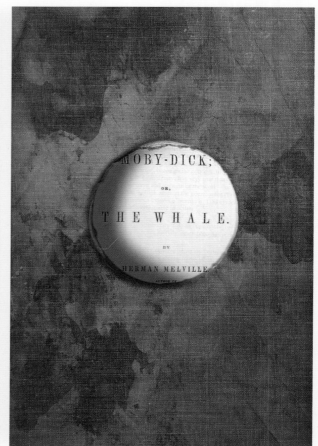
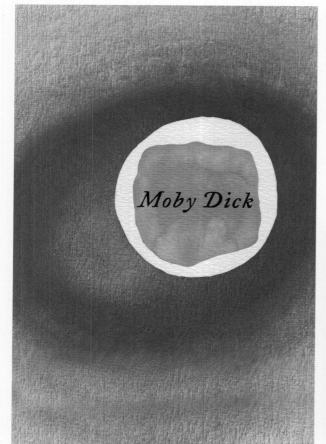
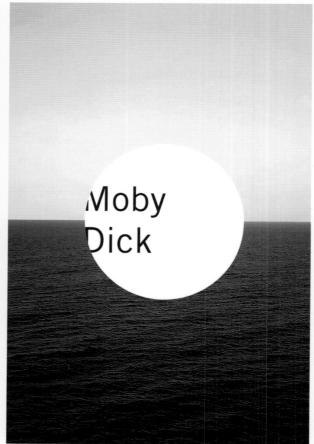

Moby-Dick explorations by Peter Mendelsund: the void.

Moby-Dick exploration by Peter Mendelsund: a doubloon as a prize.

MOBY DICK

Herman Melville

Melville

Moby Dick

太宰治

7. The Future of the Book Cover

Consider the display table at your local bookstore. It's holding a variety of books, some lying flat on their backs, others propped up by a small stand. The books come in different shapes and sizes, with covers as diverse as they are. Some feature photographs, others are text based. Some are wildly colorful, perhaps even a little garish, while others are barely adorned at all. You've wandered in to the shop on a whim, not sure what you're looking for. As you scan the display, suddenly a book cover catches your eye. You pick it up—and voilà! You've found the one thing that you didn't even know you wanted.

Serendipity is familiar to book lovers everywhere. Horace Walpole, English writer and art historian, coined the term "serendipity" in 1754 to characterize unexpected "discoveries" made by "accidents & sagacity."[100] In more modern usage, the term is nearly synonymous with chance, for it denotes any random happy occurrence. However, Walpole insisted on the close relationship between chance and design, accident *and* sagacity. While it might seem like you just stumbled across the perfect book, it's likely that both market research and strategic thinking played a role in your experience. The staff at the bookstore will have arranged the display to increase the possibility for a serendipitous encounter, their target customer being one with an open mind and a curious eye. The book cover plays a vital role in this process. In an instant, before you've even really *noticed* it, the book must convince you to pick it up, flip it over, thumb its pages, and feel its heft—in short, to make it yours.

What is the fate of serendipity in the era of online retail? Now that most book searches start with Google and end with Amazon, it's worth wondering whether serendipitous book discovery will be displaced, like much else in contemporary culture, by algorithms and artificial intelligence. Even though independent bookstores are enjoying a resurgence, it seems that the activity of strolling the aisles or lingering at the display table belongs to a bygone era.

Or perhaps not. Take, for example, the Bohemian Bookshelf.[101] Launched by an international team of designers, the Bohemian Bookshelf is a digital tool that facilitates serendipitous book discoveries by providing a parallel to the experience of casual browsing at the brick-and-mortar store or library. Although it's common to begin searching for a book with a specific word or phrase, such as a genre label or the author's name, the Bohemian Bookshelf encourages an uncommon, less targeted approach— and, in doing so, it mobilizes the power of the book cover in a fascinating way. Once installed on a website or kiosk, the Bohemian Bookshelf enables users to navigate a collection through multiple pathways, one of which is organized entirely by color. Books in this system (which is inspired by Etsy's "Shop by Color" feature) are clustered together based on the colors of their covers, rather than on their content or genre. This means that a work of historical fiction might be adjacent to a self-help best seller. You could begin by searching for a biography of Abraham Lincoln and end up discovering a new Szechuan cookbook, simply because their respective covers share hue and saturation values.

If the Bohemian Bookshelf employs the latest digital technology to enhance an old-fashioned analog process, then it gives us a glimpse into the future of the book cover, revealing how the medium is changing in the twenty-first century. Ever since the book cover became a species of graphic design, it has been a used to visualize information and to spark curiosity. While the rise of digital technology has altered how we produce, search for, purchase, circulate, and consume books, it has not killed the physical object. Quite the opposite: according to the Pew Research Center, print books are still the most popular reading platform in the United States.[102] Meanwhile, the American Booksellers Association reports that the independent bookstore is enjoying a golden age, characterized by robust sales figures, increasing profits, and new store openings.[103] Still, digitization has elevated certain functions of the book cover over others, and it has influenced the trends, styles, and conventions of cover art.

When the designers of the Bohemian Bookshelf mention "serendipity," they're actually referring to the broader issue of discoverability. How do consumers and readers find what they don't even know they want? Web browsing, online retail, and social media have created new ways for readers to learn about titles, and the increasing number of discoverability channels has had multiple effects. On the one hand, "many customers shop for books online, primarily through Amazon, and discover books on social media, so it's most important now to create something that will be eye-catching on screens," explained Jennifer Olsen, director of digital product development at Knopf Doubleday. Typically, this means bold colors, blocky, sans-serif text, and "flat design": a minimalist style that works well across multiple platforms. While "beautifully designed and heavily produced covers may inspire a purchase," Olsen continued, "this happens less and less frequently," so "printing effects like foil and embossing are much less an impetus to purchase now than in the past."[104]

On the other hand, the *physical* book cover has become more valuable. Aiming to justify the relatively high price point of hardcovers and paperbacks compared to e-books, in recent years, designers have used special effects—such as lenticular printing, 3D imaging, stamped jackets, die cuts, spot foil or gloss, and tactilely appealing uncoated paper stock—that exploit the physicality of the tangible book. Back in the early days of e-book publishing, designers experimented with special effects for digital book covers, such as animated GIFs. However, "customers weren't especially interested, and retailers weren't supportive with merchandising or technology," Olsen said. Thus, publishers doubled their efforts to reimagine the form and function of the physical book cover.

In general, this was a welcome development for independent bookstores. As interior spaces decorated with books, indies are key sites of display for new titles "in the wild." And better-looking books mean more inviting spaces. However, when asked about the present and future of cover art, Sarah McNally, owner of McNally Jackson Books in New York City, stressed that book covers are not merely decorative objects: "I know approximately what kind of books I am open to reading, and I know approximately what kind of books I am open to featuring in my stores. Book covers give me visual cues about what sort of book I'm dealing with, in a way that jacket copy struggles to do pithily."[105]

To be sure, covers instantly convey a lot of information. Technically speaking, they are a spatial rather than a temporal art, meaning that, unlike narrative texts, films, or television shows, they don't disclose their content over an extended period of time.[106] This is why it only takes a quick glance for McNally to know whether she's dealing with "melodramatic historical fiction aimed largely at readers who like tragic tales, or historical fiction that is artful in the telling, published with gravitas and hope for awards, or any number of other sub-sub-genres." Instead of reading the blurbs and other marketing copy, she relies on the work of cover artists to inform her decisions about what to purchase for the store. "Without the work of book designers, I would go completely mad," she admitted.

No doubt, covers will continue visualizing information in the future. But like all media, they are not simply passive conduits—they play an active role in shaping how information and meaning will be received. "The more a book is asking a reader to take a chance on it, the more important the cover is," noted literary agent Chris Parris-Lamb.[107] Parris-Lamb explained that there's an inverse relationship between cover art and other marketing advantages, such as name recognition. The fewer advantages that a book has to compete in the fierce world of twenty-first-century publishing, the more important the cover design is. An author like John Grisham needs no help getting noticed, but if the author is unknown, or the topic of the book is obscure, the cover must work hard to carve out a niche for the product, build an audience, and shape the book's reception.

This is a way of saying that covers provide both literal and metaphorical edges. They allow us to grasp a book as a discrete thing—a node of information, meaning, and value—in a networked world of mash-ups and remixes, where everything seems to bleed into everything else. According to writer and digital designer Craig Mod, "edges are a critical framing aid in helping us *consume*," precisely because they set limits around content. "It's one reason," Mod says, "it feels so good to scroll down to 'most-emailed' stories on nytimes.com—it's bounded, doesn't update much, and you feel like you can read it all."[108] But edges are no less important to *creation*, a lesson that Mod learned as he was helping to design Flipboard for iPhone: an app that gathers news, popular stories, and social media conversations into an individually curated feed. Much like the Bohemian Bookshelf, Flipboard uses covers, broadly defined, to organize and visualize data, to frame content, and to provide the boundaries necessary for focused attention. If we're all "reading against noise," as literature scholars Deidre Shauna Lynch and Evelyne Ender have argued, then covers help to silence the din by placing edges around a text.[109]

And yet, as Mod and his colleagues were completing Flipboard, he felt a sense of loss. He asked himself, "What had we created?" One answer: "an app in the Apple iOS App Store—something representing the top slice of tremendous work." Another equally valid answer: "997 design comps in a shared folder; 9,695 git commits; a bundle of notebooks full of sketches, and dozens of photographs from launch night." In other words, a documentation of the process, a pile of *stuff*, weighing in at exactly eight pounds. Wanting to preserve all this—to memorialize the process, to draw edges around it—Mod made a book, titled *Flipboard for iPhone the Book*, and had it printed on demand and shipped to the office. When he dropped his creation on the table during the post-launch debrief, he later recalled, "you could feel the room swell with a strange relief. Finally, there were edges to this intensely immaterial process we had all been through. The book represented … closure on a process that often has no closure."

It's a nice irony: the work of designing the digital future of reading captured by the ancient technology of the codex. And what this irony illustrates is the coexistence—and perhaps even codependence—of residual and emergent media, old and new technologies for preserving and transmitting content. After all, one medium does not simply replace another, as scholar Lisa Gitelman has argued; instead, media converge, fuse, morph, evolve, and compete for strategic advantages, as organisms within the ecology of culture.[110] Book covers are increasingly used as status symbols and lifestyle signifiers on social media. At

the same time, they feature tweets-as-endorsements by celebrities and luminaries. Yet even as the book cover is being reimagined in our time, when the look of the book matters as never before, there are signs of the past everywhere. Some of the most interesting book design of this century taps into the rich traditions of Modernism and twentieth-century book art.[111] Jeffrey Schnapp, director of the metaLAB at Harvard University, has pointed out the rise of "digital era books that double down on their analog physicality."[112]

Indeed, many new initiatives in contemporary book culture have one eye on the future and the other on the past. Take, for example, "Insta Novels": a program that adapts classic works of literature, such as *Alice's Adventures in Wonderland* or "The Yellow Wallpaper," for the Instagram Stories platform. Working with the design firm Mother, the New York Public Library launched Insta Novels in 2018 with the goal of bringing great literature to Instagram's four hundred million daily users.[113] While it might seem like a text-based art form has no place on a photo-sharing application, the designers found innovative ways to make each narrative both legible and delightful for the user. "Every single part of the design was tailored to make the story the most entertaining, to make it the most simple to use, and make it the most natural within the environment of Instagram," explains Corinna Falusi, partner and chief creative officer at Mother.[114] The text, neither too small nor too large, rests against a warm cream background that is easy on the eyes. Sprinkled throughout the narrative are small animations that enhance the text. And every story opens with a kind of book cover: an original design that gives the classic title a new look. By all accounts, the project has been successful. The Library estimates that about three hundred million people now read books this way.

Even though these stories are in the public domain, and are therefore freely accessible in text-only formats via websites such as Project Gutenberg, readers still care about how their books are packaged. This insight is driving another innovative project at the intersection of literature and design: the release of classic titles, presented in fresh ways, on

Apple Books, *Moby-Dick* by Herman Melville, design by Oliver Munday and Peter Mendelsund.

Le joueur d'échecs
Stefan Zweig

La coscienza di Zeno
Italo Svevo

La métamorphose
Franz Kafka

Alice's Adventures in Wonderland
Lewis Carroll

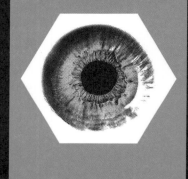

Frankenstein
Mary Shelley

Les Fleurs du mal
Baudelaire

Fables de La Fontaine

The Jungle Book
Rudyard Kipling

Don Juan Tenorio
José Zorrilla

Apple Books covers by Peter Mendelsund and Oliver Munday.

Apple Books. Beginning with freely available texts such as Guy de Maupassant's "Le Horla," Charles Baudelaire's *Les Fleurs du Mal*, and Franz Kafka's *La Métamorphose*, Apple enlisted a design team to give each work a striking new cover so that readers who download the book from the Apple Books store can have an aesthetically pleasing experience. "We worked with a team of dedicated editors, designers, and marketers," explains one of the cover artists, Oliver Munday. "The goal was to create a distinct series look, so that the series is branded and unified—and thus appeals to completists—while allowing for each individual title to retain its character. It was important for us that these covers faithfully represent individual texts, while adhering to the series architecture as a whole."[115]

Although this project includes approximately a hundred titles, a fair amount of the time designing was spent on *Moby-Dick*. "There are so many versions of the *Moby-Dick* cover," Munday rued. "Our first drafts attempted to capture the encyclopedic nature of the book, but we found that this approach lacked a sense of pathos, emotion, or humanity." Eventually, the designers agreed to put a human figure on the cover—perhaps it's Ishmael or Ahab or an amalgam of the two characters—somewhat obscured by a whale's tail. "The use of the tail partially occludes the face on the cover, such that [the human figure] retains a degree of abstraction and universality." It is a fitting visual signifier for a novel that is both hyperspecific and immensely capacious.

So, what is the future of the book cover? Perhaps this is the wrong question, since the book cover seems to have many possible futures. Whether physical or digital, it will continue to visualize and communicate information, and it will provide edges around the text, thereby framing the reading experience as bounded and discrete. But as we have suggested throughout this book, covers do more than perform these basic tasks. They *translate* verbal art into visual form. They *interpret* the texts that they envelope. They *remediate* other media, like photographs. They *connect* people, institutions, and cultural forces. They *assert* the value of long-form writing in an era of tweets, even as they *do whatever they can* to capture attention in an age of distraction. They *beautify* our homes and *signify* our interests and desires. They *concretize* the abstract zone where text meets context, showing through their styles and trends how literature interacts with an ever-changing culture. And more.

Because the book cover does so much work, perhaps we ought to follow the example of cultural theorist Raymond Williams in thinking about its future. Williams urged us to see the "dominant, residual, and emergent" roles of any cultural product.[116] If the Bohemian Bookshelf, Flipboard, Insta Novels, and Apple Books represent emerging futures for the book cover, then these designs build on the cover's residual function, its analog physicality. And if there's growing interest in books as objects and indie bookstores as temples of expertly curated content, then this interest is no doubt a reaction against the frantic churn of contemporary life.

One thing is certain: the book cover is always evolving, and as it continues to do so, it will continue shedding light on the shifting relationships among literature, culture, design, technology, media, and the economy. Indeed, the book cover is a prime example of what poet Ezra Pound called a "luminous detail": a bright spot, in a crowded cultural field, that enables us to see the world in a fresh way.[117] That is, if we pause long enough to ponder it.

"A great book cover is, for me, like a great Spanish edition. The designer takes the manuscript and deftly translates it into a language I understand, but am unable to speak with any clarity. *How on earth did you do that?* I think when I'm given the finished product. To take 70,000 words, and turn them into a single image. How is that not a miracle?"

—David Sedaris, author

8. CONCLUSION: Conversations at the Edge

A cover can make or break the launch of a book, so when it comes time to decide which prototype to green-light, the stakes are high. But what really happens behind the scenes? How do the covers that appear on real or virtual bookshelves ultimately win approval? "A big-time corporate cover meeting can seem like a therapy session," reports designer John Gall. "You don't like green? Go on …"[118] As the creative director at Alfred A. Knopf, Gall has participated in his share of such meetings, which involve any number of stakeholders with varying levels of expertise, as well as different—and perhaps also competing—priorities. "One person's job might depend on the book being taken seriously as literature," for example, "while another person's job is to get books into Costco." Accordingly, as designer Janet Hansen explains, the approval process can be "surprisingly grueling."

Indeed, even if book covers prompt ambivalent feelings, everyone seems to agree that they matter, which means that everyone seems to have an opinion about them. When he gives lectures on his design process, Gall displays an infographic that documents what a cover would look like if he had incorporated all the suggestions offered to him along the way—the various notes from the publisher, associate publisher, editor, editor in chief, managing editor, editorial assistants, sales and marketing professionals, publicity people, author's agent, author's family and friends, and even the author's psychic! That sounds like a lot of feedback, but experienced designers are used to it. "At any given time," Hansen rues, "designers can be found battling off uninspired requests" from just about anyone.

Meanwhile, where is the author in all this? Usually struggling to be heard above the din of new voices that have been introduced at this late stage of the book production process. "You let the text go," explains novelist Claire Messud. "The designers do their thing, and if you're offended, you squawk." Like others in her position, Messud reports that she can influence, but not determine, the final outcome. "I've sort of lost a say in how my books look, although I can throw a tantrum if I hate something, and they'll change it." Novelist and photography critic Teju Cole has a similar attitude about the process and its participants. "Book design is professionalized," he realizes. "It isn't just, 'Oh, I want this or that on the cover of my book!' No. There are people within the publishing house whose job is to make this decision for you—and to persuade you, really. I just learned to respect their expertise."

Throughout *The Look of the Book*, we have argued that covers are connectors in both the literal and the metaphorical sense. They are truly social media, for they bring together otherwise disparate people, ideas, desires, and demands. Poised on the cusp between art and commerce, they occasion intense scrutiny and serious debate about how they should look and feel, what they should do, and what makes them successful as aesthetic objects, marketing devices, and user interfaces. And yet it's conventional for authors and designers to toil away in separate silos, or to have their interactions mediated by a third party such as an editor. Even if the final approval meeting is the slightly raucous affair that Gall and Hansen describe, it's likely that the cover designer and the author will have had limited contact up to that point. Novelist Rachel Kushner goes so far as to call it a "firewall between the book designer and the person who wrote the book."

Although there are valid reasons for this separation of powers—designers, just like writers, must be wary of too much meddling from others—we initially pitched *The Look of the Book* as an experiment in collaboration. What, we wondered, could writers and designers learn from one another? And how might such learning reorient our understanding of the ways that book culture is changing in the digital era? To explore these questions, we conducted dozens of interviews, gleaning insights that informed our thinking from start to finish. As a fitting conclusion to this book, therefore, we envisioned a kind of symposium: a dialogue about the various themes raised in the preceding chapters, a conversation across the gulf that separates authors from designers. But it was impractical, if not impossible, to get all of our interviewees into the same room together. Designers are busy designing, writers are busy writing, and the rest of us—readers all—are eagerly awaiting the fresh fruits of their labor.

So, instead of convening an actual symposium, we turned to a technique in design research known as affinity mapping.[119] It's a simple but powerful way to discover shared themes among different interviewees, while probing beneath the surface of what people say in order to understand what they really mean. Whether conversing with designers, authors, or other publishing professionals, certain themes surfaced repeatedly—taste, mediation, process, and book fetishism, to name a few—and the longer we worked on this project, the more convinced we became of the need to listen closely and critically to what we talk about when we talk about book covers, for these seemingly trivial things nonetheless provoke a wide range of nontrivial feelings and thoughts.[120]

"I am struck by the paradox," critic James Wood confesses, "of my not reflecting very much on book covers generally and that at the same time, like most people, I have fairly strong likes and dislikes, opinions, and so on." These opinions were formed early on. "I have in my own aesthetic response to books," Wood continues, "a kind of snobbery that comes from two things. One was that my early teenage reading was paperback poetry and volumes of poetry, particularly when they were done in a uniform Faber edition, tending to have no illustration at all. What I liked about them, precisely, was just the thought that had gone into the lettering. There was a certain magnificent austerity about that, which, for me, was also attractive."

"Publishers and editors have relinquished literary taste and publishing judgment to the yahoos." —Lawrence Ratzkin, designer, letter to the editor, *New York Times*

From the outside, such attraction can almost look like revulsion. "I'm a real destroyer of books," Wood continues. "I think it's important to make them your own and pulverize them and dog-ear and write in them and drop them in the bath and all that." Interestingly enough, though, Wood has "no instinct to do any of this with a hardback," perhaps because hardbacks are usually more valuable than their counterparts. And when it comes to literary fiction, questions of value are never far from view—"everybody," as Cole puts it, "is worried about looking highbrow"—even if one is browsing for books at Costco, amid discounted flat-screens and tube socks.

Of course, there's no accounting for taste, and one person's "magnificent austerity" is another person's lazy lack of decoration. Is there a happy medium? For Messud, it's all about the details of book production. "As a student, I spent a summer working at Viking Penguin in New York," she recalls, "and I worked for the managing editor. This is in the late '80s. At that time, the managing editor was making these decisions about every single book that they were producing. I was aware of all the decisions that went into designing a book, because of that summer job, and I cared a huge amount. I felt absolutely invested in the physical design of the book. It wasn't just the cover that was important to me; it was the paper stock, it was the end papers, it was the typeface and everything else."

Comparing that time to our present moment, Messud laments that we have lost an appreciation for "the dignity of small things." By contrast, it was a certain kind of *bigness* that struck novelist Tom McCarthy the first time that he visited the New York office of his publisher, Penguin Random House. "It's like stepping into a cathedral. You've got all these huge walls of glass with books and little shrines right behind them, going back to the '40s, when companies like this started. It's really nice to see the covers from the '50s and '60s, just to see the brilliance of the design. They're so, so good."

Kushner appreciates this earlier aesthetic, too, but she places a premium on novelty. "I feel like designers should make new things look like new things," she remarks, "rather than copying mid-century tastefulness." Of course, most designers would agree, but

they would also stress that "the odds for a great jacket are sometimes stacked against us," as Hansen puts it. This is not only because key decision-makers occasionally choose "uninspired" ideas; it's also because of technological and commercial constraints. "Amazon hoisted the thumbnail image to supremacy," carps designer Oliver Munday. "Imagine your grand ambition reduced to the size of postage." In the same breath, however, Munday cautions against nostalgia for the bygone days of cover design: "It's tempting to look back on the precomputer age when the likes of George Salter created a cover's every element. In retrospect, it almost seems like art, but the humble designer is alive to the perils of believing himself an artist. Artists create in isolation, free from external directives. Artists flout approval."

Still, the collaborative nature of design does have an upside. "If we understand writers as the artists in our scenario," Munday explains, "this allows for something interesting to happen. It turns designers into *interpreters* of art, our work into a kind of inverted ekphrasis where dramatic visuals are divined from the text. It can feel like magic." Speaking from an author's perspective, McCarthy agrees. "The best book designers, like Suzanne Dean, with whom I work in the UK, are very good at not literally 'illustrating' the book. Instead, they'll deconstruct the narrative and cut it right down to the kind of images, the source images that may not actually be evident on the surface, that are toiling away behind the surface. And they'll bring those up into visibility. And it's almost alchemy. I'm always amazed at the genius involved."

Whether it's called "magic," "alchemy," or "genius," cover design has never been more important than it is today. Like everything else, books must compete for our time against a seemingly endless array of digital distractions, and their covers are on the front line of the attention war raging across social and mobile media.[121] While it might seem like a bad time for books, a longer view of history helps to put this moment into perspective. "The book," as writer and artist Craig Mod reminds us, "has been usurped a dozen times over by radio, TV, movies, and then a hundred times over by smartphones. Smartphones are so powerful we can't look away." Nonetheless, as a lover of *physical* books, Mod is sanguine about the future: "I certainly don't think that physical books are going anywhere soon, but I do hope that enough of a readership is present to fund the industry." He suggests that the right path forward for "the codex in the face of the digital" is to "double down" on what makes the codex so special—above all, its ability to "aid deep focus and concentration."

Likewise, McCarthy has no patience for hand-wringing over the decline, or supposed decline, of books and book culture. "We always naturalize whatever form of media we grow up with and think it's real," he asserts, "and then the next one is just some kind of betrayal of that. In twenty years' time, we're going to be telling our kids to stop wasting time with whatever new medium there is." To be sure, it's easy to imagine the parents of the future

scolding their tweens: "Why don't you look at a proper laptop or something!?"

The dynamics of media relations—how verbal, visual, physical, and virtual media interact, compete, and cross-pollinate—have always intrigued McCarthy as a novelist, for these dynamics are central to the history of that literary form. "If you look back to the earliest novels, something like *Robinson Crusoe* is absolutely obsessed with its own materiality. Crusoe spends so much time deliberating on his ink supplies. Samuel Richardson asks, 'How am I going to get paper to write this manuscript?' In *Don Quixote*, you see Quixote and Panza at the beginning of the second book looking at the book itself as an object, saying: 'I don't like this bit, and the form it comes in.'" This history matters, McCarthy argues, even though "the internet

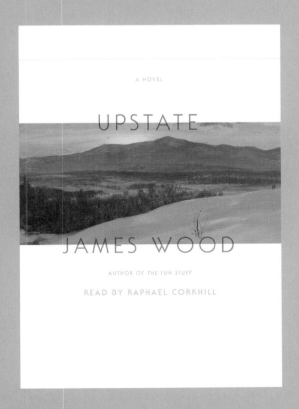

Upstate by James Wood, cover by
Janet Hansen, 2018.

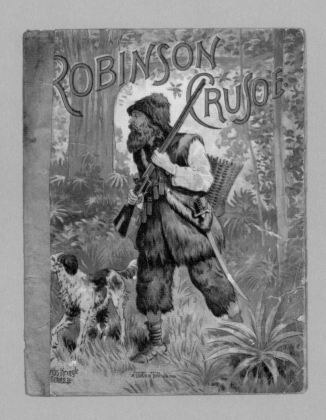

Robinson Crusoe by Daniel Defoe,
illustrated edition, McLoughlin
Bros, 1897.

is generating the world's data" and "the world is writing itself now," because novels have always understood themselves as impossible, obsolete forms of art. "To go back again to *Don Quixote*: the whole premise of the novel is that the novel doesn't work."

This is a way of saying that "the novel has always been new media and has always been aware of itself as new media," inextricably bound up with other cultural and aesthetic forms, including books and book covers, which McCarthy calls "the indebted, the unhallowed souls in the limbo zone between art and commerce." And speaking of covers, Cole offers a different but equally suggestive metaphor: "I think book covers are a little bit like soundtracks in films. Most soundtracks are inoffensive, and they're pretty bad in the sense that they're sort of all replaceable with each other. They're emotional cues, and they're telling you what to think as you watch the film. And then you encounter a really good soundtrack, and you almost want to weep because you're like, 'Why can't they all be like this?'" What he means, in other words, is that "a great cover" is "evocative without being closed, inviting without being cloying."

Take, for example, the cover for Cole's *Open City* (2011). Designed to convey what the book's editor called the "fever dream" quality of the narrative, the yellow color scheme gives the cover a strong visual presence. "It's striking and legible, no matter how small you make it," Cole avers. Initially, however, he had wanted to use a photograph as the centerpiece of the design, but his publisher suggested otherwise. "If we use a photograph," he recalls his editor telling him, "people will get the idea that *Open City* is a nonfiction book." In the end, even though the final design wasn't Cole's favorite, he had to admit that his editor was right. "Suddenly, the yellow cover became something that people would see everywhere, and they would know that they had seen it before. The cover established a strong visual identity. Do I love it now? Do I think it was perfect for the book? I don't know, because now it's just so much a part of the book's identity for me."

Le Corbusier's personal copy of *Don Quixote* by Miguel de Cervantes, bound in the pelt of his beloved schnauzer, Pinceau. *Opposite: Open City* by Teju Cole, cover by Lynn Buckley.

OPEN
CITY

TEJU COLE

a novel

"Superb . . . Scintillatingly alive . . . A pure explosion of now." –THE NEW YORKER
"Electric . . . Addictive . . . Smart and satisfying." –O, THE OPRAH MAGAZINE

THE FLAME THROWERS

10 BEST BOOKS
The New York Times Book Review 2013

NATIONAL BOOK AWARD FINALIST

A NOVEL

RACHEL KUSHNER

NATIONAL BOOK AWARD–NOMINATED AUTHOR OF *TELEX FROM CUBA*

"BRILLIANTLY ALIVE."
—James Wood, *The New Yorker*

"HER PROSE HAS A POISE AND WARINESS AND MORAL GRAININESS THAT PUTS YOU IN THE MIND OF WEARY-SOULED VISIONARIES LIKE ROBERT STONE AND JOAN DIDION."
—DWIGHT GARNER, *THE NEW YORK TIMES BOOK REVIEW*

The STRANGE CASE OF RACHEL K

RACHEL KUSHNER

"Kushner is the champion of something strange, wonderful, and real."—Rivka Galchen

'Scintillatingly alive'
JAMES WOOD, *NEW YORKER*

'One of the most thrilling and high-octane literary experiences I have had in ages'
COLUM MCCANN, *SUNDAY INDEPENDENT*

THE FLAME THROWERS RACHEL KUSHNER

Covers of Rachel Kushner books. *Clockwise from top left: The Flamethrowers*, Farrar Straus and Giroux, cover by Charlotte Strick *The Strange Case of Rachel K*, New Directions cover by Paul Sahre *The Flamethrowers* Harvill Secker, cover by Suzanne Dean

Opposite bottom: The Mars Room by Rachel Kushner unused cover comp by Peter Mendelsund. Kushner had voiced her admiration for the covers of the French publisher Gallimard (*opposite top*)

Kushner describes a similar give-and-take in her experience with *The Flamethrowers* (2013). "I went to New York to meet with the designer," she explains. "I showed him the image that I had: an archival photo of a real woman from an underground leftist magazine in Rome in the late 1970s, and everybody automatically said, 'Oh, you can't have a photograph of a person on a novel, because people will be confused, and they will conflate her image with the voice of the narrator.'" Eventually, however, the publisher agreed to use the photograph that appears on the final jacket: the striking close-up of a woman with tape over her mouth. Kushner credits the cover designer, Charlotte Strick, with bringing it all together through her use of just the right typeface. "I could never have imagined that typeface; it was absolutely brilliant ingenuity of the book designer, and without that, you don't have much. If you just have the image, it's raw material that could indicate the direction of a good-looking book, but it's not enough. I think of it as a collaboration, although obviously it's one hundred percent her brilliance."

The best part for Kushner, moreover, was how Strick's design caused her to see *The Flamethrowers* in a new way. "I didn't really think much about the implications of the fact that in the photograph, the woman has tape over the mouth. The irony is that the book is four hundred pages of her speaking to the reader and being drowned out by various men in various rooms." When it came time for Kushner to consider the designs for her next book, *The Mars Room* (2018), she was already open to the possibility that the process would be collaborative. When she submitted the manuscript, "the title was not settled upon," so it was interesting to play with different options while considering the overall design of the cover. "I wanted to know what the designer thought of the title, since the title, obviously, would indicate the possibilities for different paths, visually. I sent him a bunch of images. He sent me images. We talked about covers of books that we really liked."

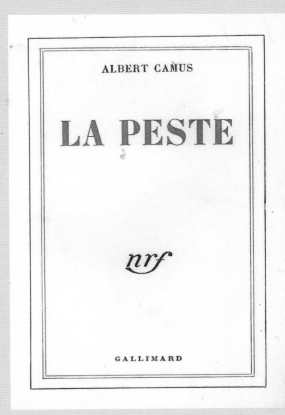

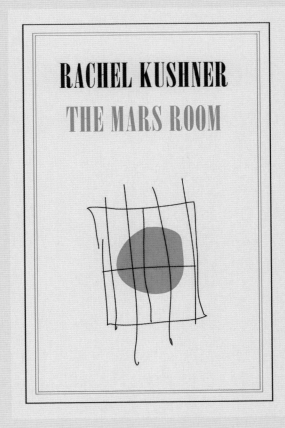

RACHEL KUSHNER

THE MARS ROOM

A NOVEL

THE AUTHOR OF THE FLAMETHROWERS

I wanted to know what the designer thought of the title, since the title, obviously, would indicate the possibilities for different paths, visually." —Rachel Kushner

Rachel Kushner The Mars Room

Rachel
Kushner's
*The Mars
Room,* unused
cover comps
by Peter
Mendelsund.
Opposite:
Confinement
and escape.
This page:
Bars and the
red planet.

McCarthy suspects that there might be a secret plan guiding how this process unfolds. "You go into the office after a couple weeks, and they show you maybe three or four different ideas," he explains. "And I'm guessing they stagger it, so they show you the one they don't want first. They work you up to the one they actually want." Clever presentation tactics, however, have yet to detract from McCarthy's experience. "It's very interesting. Even the covers that don't end up being used. Between them, the four or five of them, they make a whole constellation, the image repertoire of the book. It's really exhilarating seeing that kind of step-by-step process and moving up to that."

It makes sense that designers would need to be savvy (if not also a little cagey) during the approval process, because "in the end," as Gall rues, "no one knows if a particular cover design is going to make a book successful." And what is "successful" anyway? For Messud, it's "something that's familiar, but a little different. If something is too different, that's a challenge. So there's a logic to it, but a really simple logic." Of course, success and failure are relative terms, highly contingent upon cultural and historical circumstances. If ours is a time of increasing social and cultural division, then it is also a time of false connection, fake intimacy, and what Cole calls "artificial proximity." He insists that we push back against the "epidemic of relatability" that has besieged book culture. "It's like everybody wants to be 'fun,' but not all books are 'fun.'"

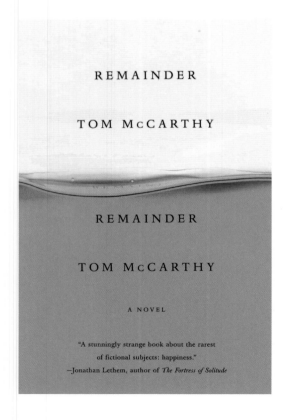

"It's like everybody wants to be 'fun,' but not all books are 'fun.'"

John Gall's cover for *Remainder* by Tom McCarthy. *Opposite: The Lennon Play* by John Lennon, Adrienne Kennedy, and Victor Spinetti; cover by Lawrence Ratzkin.

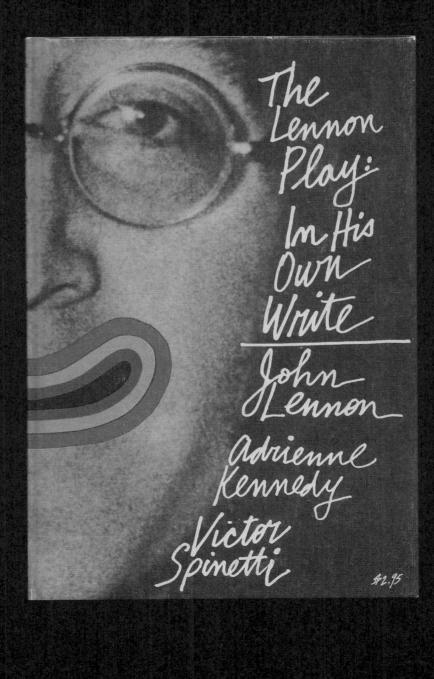

No, not all books are fun. Rather, they're as diverse as the people who make them: the authors, the designers, and the other publishing professionals who have a hand in what appears, season after season, for the readers and bibliophiles of the world. And while it's easy to dismiss book covers as superficial and ancillary, we hope that *The Look of the Book* has convinced you of their significance—their power to ...

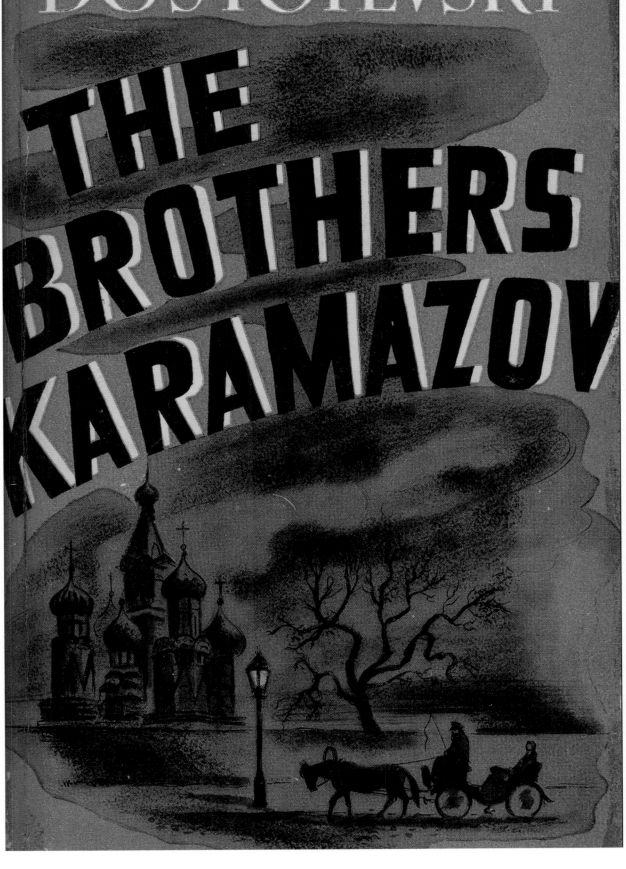

DOSTOYEVSKY

THE BROTHERS KARAMAZOV

95¢

THE
THIN
MAN
DASHIELL
HAMMETT

CRIME

ALAIN ROBBE-GRILLET
THE VOYEUR

FAWCETT
PREMIER
M491•95c

ISAAC ASIMOV presents
two science fiction novels by
H. G. WELLS
The Time Machine
The War of the Worlds

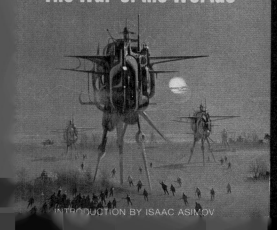

INTRODUCTION BY ISAAC ASIMOV

THOMAS MANN
THE MAGIC
MOUNTAIN

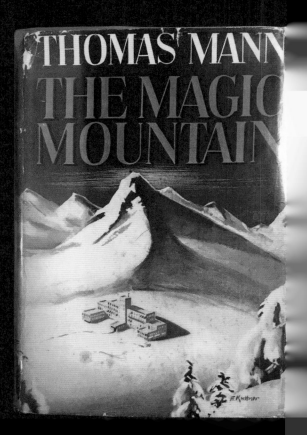

interpret texts

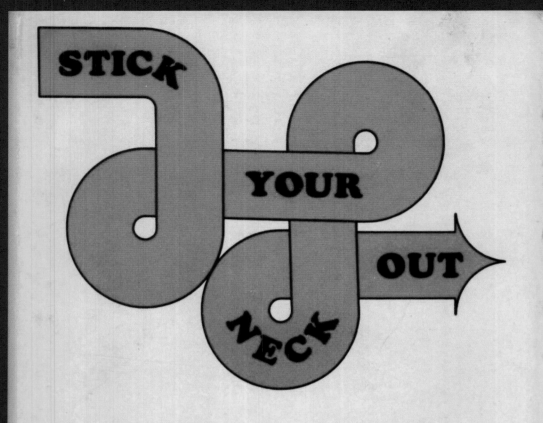

STICK YOUR NECK OUT

by Mordecai Richler

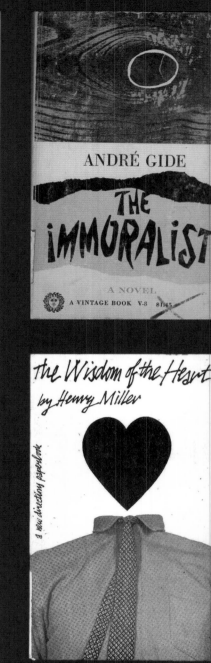

ANDRÉ GIDE
THE IMMORALIST
A NOVEL
A VINTAGE BOOK V-8 $1.45

the Wisdom of the Heart
by Henry Miller

a new directions paperbook

DELIVERANCE
A NOVEL BY
JAMES DICKEY

MOONRAKER

IAN
FLEMING

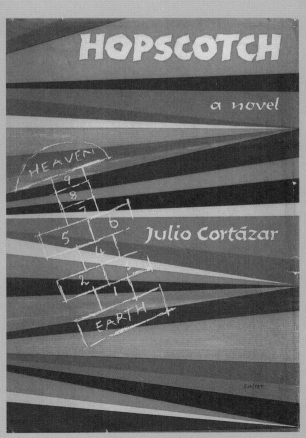

HOPSCOTCH

a novel

Julio Cortázar

REUNION &
REACTION

C. VANN WOODWARD

The story of how Northern Republicans and Southern
Democrats joined together in 1877, ending the era
of Reconstruction, and forming the basis for the
powerful conservative coalitions that were to influence American politics for generations to come.
SECOND EDITION, REVISED

A DOUBLEDAY ANCHOR BOOK

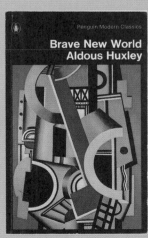

Penguin Modern Classics

Brave New World
Aldous Huxley

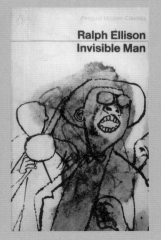

Penguin Modern Classics

Ralph Ellison
Invisible Man

The
White

Virgin
ORL

and, at their best ...

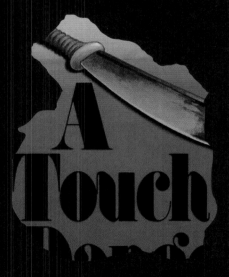

A
Touch

ren of t

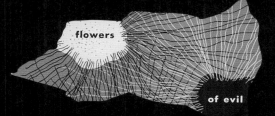

flowers

of evil

AWEIK
ROSLAV
ASEK

bring people
together.

ONLY
TWICE

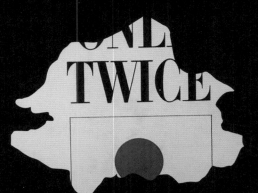

Flesh

BY PAUL V. RUSS

Son
OF

Glossary

Unless otherwise noted, all definitions have been adapted from the Oxford English Dictionary *and John Carter and Nicolas Barker's* ABC for Book Collectors.

BISAC CODE – Literally "Book Industry Standards and Communications," these subject headings enact categories into which published materials are slotted or tagged. As part of a system of classification, BISAC codes condition reader and bookseller expectations. Like genres, they exist in tension with published texts, as neither fully determines the other. Importantly, multiple BISAC codes join together as descriptive layers for a given book. Three codes is the industry standard for a published work, though the first code listed has the greatest impact on "shelving," determining where in a retail space or library a physical book will be placed or how it will be categorized or tagged in a digital database.

BLURB – Originally slang, this term describes the verbal enticements on a book's jacket or cover that constitute part of its paratext. Blurbs are laudatory, canned, or categorical, and they are a component of overall jacket design. Sometimes they make a claim for a book's competency by excerpting the comments of an expert or authority. Blurbs began to circulate widely in the United States during the 1920s and 1930s.

BOARD – The hardback casings between which a book's pages reside. The term, evocative of wood's solidity, can refer to any hard cover, which, in the past, sometimes featured decorations or embellishments. Today, the detachable book jacket, which emerged in the 1820s, serves to clothe the boards. Initially, jackets were designed to reproduce the look of decorated boards. If one were to extend the sartorial metaphor of the book jacket, the board is akin to the human body. Originally, boards were considered only temporary housing for a finished book, until it could be bound in leather by a professional binder, usually hired by the book's purchaser. In recent years, publishing has seen something of a return to "paper-over-board," or printed books sold without a jacket and with any design elements or embellishments appearing directly on the paper that forms the outermost layer of the board itself.

CLOTH, PUBLISHER'S CLOTH – By the mid-nineteenth century, publishers had become accustomed to binding in cloth, or casing, a practice that shifted the cost of preserving a book from the purchaser to the publisher. This process involved using canvas or other inexpensive cloth to wrap the boards and spine. Like boards, publisher's cloth was originally conceived as a temporary binding, but it soon became the norm to leave one's books cased in cloth. This gave rise to the adornment of cloth covers by publishers to differentiate between books being sold. A cloth's texture, grain, and color were thoroughly considered in designing the look and feel of a book. Cloths were sometimes embossed or otherwise made to mimic leather. The book jacket emerged around the time that publishers began using cloth.

COLOPHON – Derived from its original meaning (i.e., a finishing touch or final flourish), this term refers to the inscription and symbols indicating the title, the scribe or printer's name, and the date and location of printing. Historically, this information was placed on the final page of the book, hence the phrase "from title page to colophon." Since roughly the sixteenth century, though, these items have shifted to the title page at the beginning of the edition. The term is also used to refer solely to the publisher's symbol or logo that appears on a book's spine.

CODEX – This term refers to the format of published books, which typically feature stacked pages bound on one side. Replacing the scrolls of the ancient world, the codex has been reinvented over centuries to meet the publishing demands of a given period.

DECKLED EDGE – The effect whereby a sheet of paper has a rough-cut, untrimmed edge, giving it a handmade look. The "deckle" is the part of the machinery that controls the size and thickness of the paper during manufacture. Deckled edges lend an antiquarian feel to a modern book and contribute to a book's overall design. Typically more expensive than conventionally cut edges in contemporary printing practices, the enthusiasm for creating deckled edges on a modern book has been coined "deckle-fetishism" by book collectors and historians.

EKPHRASIS – An artistic convention wherein a verbal representation conjures a visual representation. For example, in the *Iliad*, Homer provides a detailed description of Achilles's shield as a microcosm of the cosmos. The term "reverse ekphrasis" refers to an image that is created as an interpretation of written text. The cover artist performs reverse ekphrasis.

ENDPAPERS – The blank leaves of paper found at the beginning and end of a book. The outermost layer is often adhered to the cover, known as the "pastedown," while the inner layers are bound pages. Historically, they could be patterned, textured, or include advertisement for the publisher. In modern book design, the endpapers may feature text such as blurbs, sell copy, and author biographies, or illustrations such as maps, genealogies, or decorative patterns.

ERGODIC LITERATURE – Coined by Espen Aarseth in 1997, the term "ergodic" draws on the Greek terms for "worth" and "path" to name literature in which "nontrivial effort is required" on the part of the reader. For Aarseth, this effort is not specific to any given medium. Ergodic literature requires readers to co-construct the texts they read.

GENRE, GENRE FICTION – A genre is a loosely defined category of literature, such as "epic" or "romance." Readers of a book arrive with a certain set of expectations conditioned by its genre, but genres are flexible rather than rigid designators. Texts gain meaning by responding to and developing within genres, and, likewise, genres respond to what authors are presenting, writing, and publishing. The distinction between literature and genre fiction is becoming difficult to maintain. While genre fiction used to mean horror, fantasy, science fiction, mystery, and books with mass readership, literary authors now draw on it for conventions, tropes, characters, and settings.

JACKET – The first book jackets emerged in the 1820s as protective coverings for decorative boards (i.e., hardback books). Over the next century, they became the object of illustration themselves. Importantly, jackets are both visual images and physical things.

LENTICULAR PRINTING – The publishing practice of producing an image that appears to have more dimension and depth than a flat surface. Lenticular printing can make the cover of a book seem to be almost 3D, catching the reader's eye by looking different as it's viewed from different angles and causing the image to appear animated. "Lenticular" is defined literally as pertaining to a lens or the lens of the eye.

MEDIUM – A complex term that has acquired meanings over time. In this book, we use "medium" to refer to any channel of communication (e.g., newspapers, television, radio) and to any material of artistic creation (e.g., enamel, marble, paper). The book cover is a medium in this sense. Mediation is the process whereby signals and meanings are transmitted from a sender to a receiver. Remediation is the process whereby one medium consumes another, as when a book cover features a tweet as a blurb. In *Understanding Media* (1964), Marshall McLuhan posits that a medium shapes a human experience not only through the content it delivers, but, more important, through its structure and form.

MODERNISM – A catchall term for a philosophical, cultural, and aesthetic movement that emerged as a break from tradition in the late nineteenth century. Modernism swept across many areas of art and culture, including book design and cover art. As Ned Drew and Paul Sternberger point out in *By Its Cover: Modern American Book Cover Design* (2005), the mid-twentieth century in America saw the adaptation of Euro-Modernist ideas by American designers that resulted in the "sophisticated integration of type and image." Movements such as Cubism, Dadaism, and Futurism were refracted through the lens of graphic design to create a formal visual language that favored "purified geometries."

PAPERBACK – A book bound in stiff paper or flexible card ("wrappers"), whether decorated or plain, as distinguished from the hardback or hardcover. Though rare paperback books have been dated to the fifteenth century, they gained momentum beginning in the late eighteenth century. The format was pioneered by the German Tauchnitz publishing house and later by Allen Lane of Penguin in England. Less expensive than hardcovers, paperback books are sometimes released as a later edition of a book that initially appeared in hardcover in order to boost sales with the offering of a lower price point. Alternatively, a book might be released only in paperback if it is determined that the book is more suited to bulk sale at a bargain price. The invention of cheap wood-pulp paper that resulted in the modern-day paperback is responsible for the term "pulp fiction."

PAPER STOCK, COATED/UNCOATED – Also referring to the raw material from which paper is made, the term is now used to talk about types of paper used in the making of a book and can describe paper weight (thickness) and color as well as finish. "Coated" paper stock, smoother to the touch and with a glossy, silk, or matte finish, is made when paper receives a clay coating that prevents the ink on the page from absorbing into the paper. Instead, it sits atop the clay coating, creating sharper shapes and brighter colors. "Uncoated" paper stock is paper without this coating, and while it can be made with smoother or more fibrous textures, the print on the page will have a slightly duller appearance than on coated pages, since the ink will absorb into the surface of the page.

PARATEXT – In his 1987 book *Paratexts*, literary theorist Gérard Genette defines paratext as "what enables a text to become a book." This term is used to discuss titles, forewords, epigraphs, author photos, blurbs, acknowledgments, and covers—in short, everything that connects the text to the world and to the reader. Because they work with the medium of the paratext, cover designers are paratextual artists.

POSTMODERNISM – Just as Modernism proposed a break with tradition, so too Postmodernism presumes to supersede Modernism, although its success is a matter of debate. There is no one definition of the term "Postmodernism"; in literature, it tends to designate texts published between the 1960s and 1990s that are deliberately self-conscious, that show the seams of their own construction. In *Postmodernism, or, the Cultural Logic of Late Capitalism* (1991), Fredric Jameson writes that Postmodernism treats Modernism as material to be quoted via pastiche. Consequently, one definition of Postmodernism is that it deliberately mixes media or styles. Unlike the searching, earnest affective orientation of Modernism, Postmodernism often tends toward irony and skepticism.

SLIPCASE – A made-to-measure box that snuggly fits around a book or a set of books, protecting four or five sides of the book/s and leaving one side open for easy viewing of the spine. A slipcase is one of multiple types of coverings historically used for the preservation of precious or rare editions of books.

SIGNIFIER – The material form of a sign (e.g., a sound, a printed word, an image) as distinct from its meaning. Cover artists look for signifiers in a text, then translate those signifiers from verbal to visual. What we call the "least intrusive signifier" is the detail on the cover that conveys just enough information about the text to entice the reader, without giving away any secrets about plot, character, or theme.

STAMPED JACKET – In the stamping process, a brass stamp or block is used to create a pictorial or letter impression with a press. Stamped jackets and covers might then be foil-pressed, meaning a layer of foil (often gold or silver) is adhered to the stamped design. Stamping is a different process than embossing when performed by professional bookbinders— embossing traditionally uses dye—though the results are similar, and the terms are sometimes used interchangeably.

TIMED-RELEASE QUALITY – The most ambitious book covers do not reveal all their meanings in an instant. Rather, like any successful piece of visual art, they develop significance over time and change with you as you read the book.

TRENDS AND TROPES – Tropes, in a literary or cultural context, are recurring themes or motifs. Tropes on book covers are visual cues that convey information about genre, theme, style, and form. For instance, a bloody knife signals murder mystery. Loosely tied to the content of the book, trends are tropes that are currently in fashion. Blocky text and bright colors are examples of trends in cover design at the time of this writing.

TIP SHEET – The TIP (Title and Information Profile) sheet, also known as a sales sheet, provides an "executive summary" of a book and its author. Typically, tip sheets are drafted by editors and circulated within the publishing house and to other publishing professionals. Book designers may use a tip sheet to develop initial sketches for a cover.

Notes

Chapter 1

1. George Orwell, "In Defence of the Novel," http://orwell.ru/library/articles/novel/english/e_novel.
2. Camille Paglia, "Crisis in American Universities," http://gos.sbc.edu/p/paglia.html.
3. See David Haven Blake, *Walt Whitman and the Culture of American Celebrity* (New Haven, CT: Yale University Press, 2006).
4. "medium, n. and adj.," *OED Online*, June 2018. Oxford University Press. http://www.oed.com.ezp-prod1.hul.harvard.edu/view/Entry/115772?redirectedFrom=medium.
5. On the rich tradition of artists who treat books themselves as media for creating new aesthetic objects, see Johanna Drucker, *The Century of Artists' Books*, 2nd edition (New York: Granary Books, 2004); Garrett Stewart, *Bookwork: Medium to Concept to Object to Art* (Chicago: University of Chicago Press, 2011); and Andrew Roth et al., *Artists Who Make Books* (London: Phaidon, 2017).
6. Marshall McLuhan, *Understanding Media: The Extensions of Man* (Cambridge, MA: MIT Press, 1994), 8.
7. A. Scott Berg, *Max Perkins: Editor of Genius* (New York: New American Library, 1978), 124.
8. Immanuel Kant, *The Critique of the Power of Judgment*, trans. Paul Guyer and Eric Matthews (Cambridge: Cambridge University Press, 2000).
9. Sianne Ngai, "Theory of the Gimmick," *Critical Inquiry* 43.2 (Winter 2017): 463–505.
10. Gérard Genette, *Paratexts: Thresholds of Interpretation*, trans. Jane E. Lewin (Cambridge: Cambridge University Press, 1997), 32.
11. Tom McCarthy, *Satin Island* (New York: Knopf, 2015), 133.
12. Claude Lévi-Strauss, *The View from Afar*, trans. Joachim Neugroschel and Phoebe Hoss (Chicago: University of Chicago Press, 1992), 145–46.
13. See David Shields, *Reality Hunger: A Manifesto* (New York: Knopf, 2011).
14. Espen J. Aarseth, *Cybertext—Perspectives on Ergodic Literature* (Baltimore: Johns Hopkins University Press, 1997), 1.
15. On this tradition, see Johanna Drucker, *The Century of Artists' Books* (New York: Granary Books, 2004).

Chapter 2

16. Herman Melville, *The Piazza Tales and Other Prose Pieces, 1839–1860*, in *The Writings of Herman Melville*, ed. Harrison Hayford et al. (Evanston, IL, and Chicago: Northwestern University Press and The Newberry Library, 1987), 237–39. "A Thought on Book-Binding" was originally published in *The Literary World* on 16 March 1850.
17. The history of the book cover that we recount in this chapter has been informed by (in alphabetical order): Phil Baines, *Penguin By Design: A Cover Story, 1935–2005* (New York and London: Penguin, 2016); Kenneth Davis, *Two-Bit Culture: The Paperbacking of America* (Boston: Houghton Mifflin, 1984); Ned Drew and Paul Sternberger, *By Its Cover: Modern American Book Cover Design* (New York: Princeton Architectural Press, 2005); Jürgen Holstein, *The Book Cover in the Weimar Republic* (New York: Taschen, 2015); Keith Houston, *The Book: A Cover-to-Cover Exploration of the Most Powerful Object of Our Time* (New York: W. W. Norton, 2016); Philip B. Meggs, *A History of Graphic Design, Third Edition* (New York: John Wiley and Sons, 1998); Paula Rabinowitz, *American Pulp: How Paperbacks Brought Modernism to Main Street* (Princeton, NJ: Princeton University Press, 2013); Martin Salisbury, *The Illustrated Dust Jacket, 1920–1970* (London: Thames & Hudson, 2017); G. Thomas Tanselle, *Book-Jackets: Their History, Forms, and Use* (Charlottesville, VA: The Bibliographical Society of the University of Virginia, 2011).
18. See *Bibliographical Notes & Queries*, 1.2 (April 1935), 1.
19. Jennifer Schuessler, "Harvard Confirms Book Is Bound in Human Skin," *The New York Times*, 5 June 2014, https://artsbeat.blogs.nytimes.com/2014/06/05/harvard-confirms-book-is-bound-in-human-skin/.
20. Edith Lewis, *Willa Cather Living: A Personal Record* (Lincoln, NE: University of Nebraska Press, 1953), 109–10.
21. Alfred A. Knopf to Elmer Adler, 27 April 1927, Box 731, Folder 9, Alfred A. Knopf, Inc. Papers, The Harry Ransom Center, University of Texas.
22. On the controversy surrounding Joyce's novel, see Kevin Birmingham, *The Most Dangerous Book: The Battle for James Joyce's Ulysses* (New York: Penguin, 2014).
23. Reichl left approximately 550 3×5 index cards on which he wrote his thoughts about design. Curated by Martha Scotford, these cards appeared in the 2013 exhibition *Ernst Reichl: Wide Awake Typographer* at the Columbia Rare Books and Manuscript Library: http://www.ernstreichl.org/. All Reichl quotations are from the cards in the Columbia archive.
24. Friedrich Kittler, *Gramophone, Film, Typewriter*, trans. Geoffrey Winthrop-Young and Michael Wutz (Stanford, CA: Stanford University Press, 1999), xxxix.
25. "Alvin Lustig: Biographical Notes," 1939–40, Alvin Lustig papers, 1935-1955, Archives of American Art, Smithsonian Institution.
26. See Louis Menand, "Pulp's Big Moment," *New Yorker*, January 5, 2015.
27. See Rabinowitz, *American Pulp*.
28. Quoted in Rabinowitz, *American Pulp*, 35–37.
29. Quoted in Rabinowitz, *American Pulp*, 255–60.
30. Quoted in Menand, "Pulp's Big Moment."
31. See John B. Thompson, *Merchants of Culture: The Publishing Business in the Twenty-First Century* (London: Plume, 2013).
32. Drew and Sternberger, 105.
33. Quoted in Steven Heller, "The Man with the Big Book Look," *Print* 56, 1 (2002): 49.
34. Steven Heller, "Passionate Collagists," *Print* (September/October 1983): 47–67.
35. Hal Foster, *The Return of the Real: Art and Theory at the End of the Century* (Cambridge, MA: MIT Press, 1996).
36. Quoted in Friedrich Kittler, *Gramophone, Film, Typewriter*, trans. Geoffrey Winthrop-Young and Michael Wutz (Redwood City, CA: Stanford University Press, 1999), 200.
37. On the concept of "affordances," see Don Norman, *The Design of Everyday Things* (New York: Basic Books, 2013).
38. Interview with Sarah McNally, email, March 2019.
39. These trends and figures are reported in Margot Boyer-Dry, "Welcome to the Bold and Blocky Instagram Era of Book Covers," *Vulture*, 31 January 2019, https://www.vulture.com/2019/01/dazzling-blocky-book-covers-designed-for-amazon-instagram.html.

Chapter 3

40. Alexandra Alter, "For Kazuo Ishiguro, 'The Buried Giant' Is a Departure," *New York Times*, 19 February 2015, https://www.nytimes.com/2015/02/20/books/for-kazuo-ishiguro-the-buried-giant-is-a-departure.html?_r=0.
41. James Wood, "The Uses of Oblivion," *New Yorker*, 23 March 2015, http://www.newyorker.com/magazine/2015/03/23/the-uses-of-oblivion.
42. Glen Duncan, *The Last Werewolf* (New York: Alfred A. Knopf, 2011), 98.
43. Ibid.
44. Duncan, *The Last Werewolf*, 43.
45. See Gérard Genette, *Paratexts: Thresholds of Interpretation*, trans. Jane E. Lewin (Cambridge: Cambridge University Press, 1997).
46. For further elaboration on this point, see Elaine Scarry, *Dreaming by the Book* (Princeton, NJ: Princeton University Press, 2001).
47. Ben Stoltzfus, "Alain Robbe-Grillet and Surrealism," *MLN* 78.3 (1963): 271–77.
48. Alaine Robbe-Grillet, *For a New Novel: Essays on Fiction*, trans. Richard Howard (Evanston, IL: Northwestern University Press, 1989): 18–19.
49. Kazuo Ishiguro, *The Buried Giant* (New York: Alfred A. Knopf, 2015), 297.
50. Ishiguro, *The Buried Giant*, 284.
51. On this topic, see James A. W. Heffernan, *Museum of Words: The Poetics of Ekphrasis from Homer to Ashbery* (Chicago: University of Chicago Press, 1993).
52. Wood, "The Uses of Oblivion"; Ursula K. Le Guin, "Are they going to say this is fantasy?" http://www.ursulakleguin.com/Blog2015.html#New.
53. Ishiguro, *The Buried Giant*, 258.
54. Philip Roth, "Writing American Fiction," *Commentary*, 1 March 1961, https://www.commentarymagazine.com/articles/writing-american-fiction/.
55. Sheila Heti, "Interview with Dave Hickey," *The Believer*, November/December 2007, https://www.believermag.com/issues/200711/?read=interview_hickey.
56. Lauren Fedor, "Making 'Tattoo' Indelible," *The Wall Street Journal*, 16 July 2010.
57. For a rich account of this idea, see Peter Davidson, *The Idea of the North* (London: Reaktion Books, 2005).

58. Jorge Luis Borges, "The Argentine Writer and Tradition," *Labrynths: Selected Stories & Other Writings* (New York: New Directions, 1962), 177–86.

59. Brad Stone, *The Everything Store: Jeff Bezos and the Age of Amazon* (New York: Little, Brown and Company, 2013).

Chapter 4

60. See W. J. T. Mitchell, "Image," in *Critical Terms for Media Studies*, eds. W. J. T. Mitchell and Mark B. N. Hansen (Chicago: University of Chicago Press, 2010).

61. C. S. Peirce, "The Icon, Index, and Symbol," in *Collected Works*, vol. 2, eds. Charles Hartshorne and Paul Weiss (Cambridge, MA: Harvard University Press, 1931–58); Erwin Panofsky, *Studies in Iconology: Humanistic Themes in the Art of the Renaissance* (Oxford: Oxford University Press, 1939).

62. Peter Curl, *Designing a Book Jacket* (London and New York: The Studio Publications, 1956), 85.

63. Eugenia Williamson, "Cover Girls," *The Boston Globe*, 28 June 2014.

64. Elliot Ross, "The Dangers of a Single Book Cover: The Acacia Tree Meme and 'African Literature,'" *Africa Is a Country*, 7 May 2014; Michael Silverberg, "The Reason Every Book about Africa Has the Same Cover— And It's Not Pretty," *Quartz*, 12 May 2014.

65. Leon Wieseltier, "The Extremities of Nicholson Baker," *The New York Times*, 8 August 2004.

66. Sharon Adarlo, "Judging a Book by Its Cover: Dangerous Books," *Bookslut*, September 2004.

67. See Eric Lott, *Love and Theft: Blackface Minstrelsy and the American Working Class* (Oxford: Oxford University Press, 1993); W. E. B. Du Bois, *The Souls of Black Folk* (Chicago: A. C. McClurg, 1903), 13.

68. Sam Scott, "The Story Behind *Homegoing*," *Stanford Magazine*, 13 June 2017.

69. Interview with Oliver Munday, phone, March 2018.

70. Interview with Helen Yentus, phone, March 2018.

71. Meg Wolitzer, "The Second Shelf: On the Rules of Literary Fiction for Men and Women," *The New York Times*, 30 March 2012.

72. Thu-Huong Ha, "Why Does this Brilliant, Bestselling Book Have such a Cheesy Cover?" *Quartz*, 20 September 2015.

73. Miriam Krule, "'Dressing a Refined Story with a Touch of Vulgarity': An Interview with Elena Ferrante's Art Director," *Slate*, 28 August 2015, https://slate.com/culture/2015/08/elena-ferrante -neapolian-novels-cover-design-an-interview-with-the -publisher-or-europa-editions-on-the-books-dreamy -illustrations.html.

74. Emily Harnett, "The Subtle Genius of Elena Ferrante's Bad Book Covers," *The Atlantic*, 3 July 2016.

75. Rebecca Solnit, "80 Books No Woman Should Read," *Literary Hub*, 18 November 2015.

76. Caroline Criado Perez, *Invisible Women: Exposing Data Bias in a World Designed for Men* (New York: Abrams, 2019), 1.

77. "Invisible Women," *99% Invisible*, podcast, 23 July 2019.

78. Claire Messud, *The Woman Upstairs* (New York: Knopf, 2013), 3.

79. On this topic, see "Would You Want to Be Friends with Humbert Humbert?: A Forum on 'Likeability,'" *New Yorker*, 16 May 2013.

80. Interview with Carol Devine Carson, email, November 2019.

Chapter 5

81. Charles Rosner, *The Art of the Book-Jacket* (London: Victoria and Albert Museum, 1949), 3.

82. Quoted in William Veeder and Susan Griffin, eds., *The Art of Criticism: Henry James on the Theory and the Practice of Criticism* (Chicago: University of Chicago Press, 1986), 20.

83. James W. Heffernan, *Museum of Words: The Poetics of Ekphrasis from Homer to Ashbery* (Chicago: University of Chicago Press, 1993), 3.

84. Peter Curl, *Designing a Book Jacket* (London and New York: The Studio Publications, 1956).

85. Curl, *Designing a Book Jacket*, 7.

86. Curl, *Designing a Book Jacket*, 10.

87. On the pulp paperback revolution in the United States, see Paula Rabinowitz, *American Pulp: How Paperbacks Brought Modernism to Main Street* (Princeton, NJ: Princeton University Press, 2014).

88. Curl, *Designing a Book Jacket*, 7.

89. Margot Boyer-Dry, "Welcome to the Bold and Blocky Instagram Era of Book Covers," *Vulture*, 31 January 2019, https://www.vulture .com/2019/01/dazzling-blocky-book-covers-designed -for-amazon-instagram.html.

90. Interview with Chris Parris-Lamb, phone, February 2019.

91. Boyer-Dry, "Welcome."

92. Curl, *Designing a Book Jacket*, 7.

93. Curl, *Designing a Book Jacket*, 9.

94. Curl, *Designing a Book Jacket*, 19.

95. Curl, *Designing a Book Jacket*, 20.

96. Curl, *Designing a Book Jacket*, 29.

97. See, for example, Ellen Lupton, *Thinking with Type: A Critical Guide for Designers, Writers, Editors, Students* (Princeton, NJ: Princeton Architectural Press, 2010).

98. Curl, *Designing a Book Jacket*, 29.

99. Curl, *Designing a Book Jacket*, 30.

Chapter 7

100. "serendipity, n," *OED Online*, March 2019, Oxford University Press, http://www .oed.com.ezp-prod1.hul.harvard.edu/view /Entry/176387?redirectedFrom=serendipity (accessed April 15, 2019).

101. Alice Thudt, *The Bohemian Bookshelf*, http://www .alicethudt.de/BohemianBookshelf/.

102. Andrew Perrin, "Book Reading 2016," *Pew Research Center*, 1 September 2016, https://www.pewresearch.org /internet/2016/09/01/book-reading-2016/.

103. *American Booksellers Association*, https://www .bookweb.org/for-the-record.

104. Interview with Jennifer Olsen, email, March 2019.

105. Interview with Sarah McNally, email, March 2019.

106. Joseph Frank, "Spatial Form in Modern Literature: An Essay in Three Parts," *The Sewanee Review* 53.4 (Autumn 1945): 643–53.

107. Interview with Chris Parris-Lamb, email, February 2019.

108. Craig Mod, "The Digital-Physical: On Building Flipboard for iPhone & Finding the Edges of our Digital Narratives," https://craigmod.com/journal /digital_physical/.

109. Deidre Shauna Lynch and Evelyne Ender, "Introduction—Time for Reading," *PMLA* 133.5 (October 2018), 1073–82.

110. Lisa Gitelman, *Always Already New: Media, History, and the Data of Culture* (Cambridge, MA: MIT Press, 2006).

111. On this tradition, see Johanna Drucker, *The Century of Artist's Books*, 2nd Edition (New York: Granary Books, 2004).

112. Jeffrey Schnapp, "Doubling Down (or FuturPiaggio)," http://jeffreyschnapp.com/2017/01/07 /doubling-down-or-futurpiaggio/.

113. New York Public Library staff, "Insta Novels: Bringing Classic Literature to Instagram Stories," 22 August 2018, https://www.nypl.org/blog/2018/08/22 /instanovels.

114. Katharine Schwab, "Hundreds of Thousands of People Read Novels on Instagram. They May Be the Future," *Fast Company*, 25 September 2019, https://www .fastcompany.com/90392917/the-next-big-reading -platform-may-be-instagram.

115. Interview with Oliver Munday and Peter Mendelsund, February 2020.

116. Raymond Williams, "Dominant, Residual, and Emergent," in *Marxism and Literature* (New York: Oxford University Press, 2009), 121–8.

117. Demetres P. Tryphonopoulos and Stephen J. Adams, eds., *The Ezra Pound Encyclopedia* (Westport, CT: Greenwood Press, 2005).

Chapter 8

118. Thanks to Teju Cole, John Gall, Janet Hansen, Rachel Kushner, Tom McCarthy, Claire Messud, Craig Mod, Oliver Munday, and James Wood for participating in this project. Interviews were conducted by phone and email between 2017 and 2019.

119. For a description of this technique, see https:// www.interaction-design.org/literature/article /affinity-diagrams-learn-how-to-cluster-and-bundle -ideas-and-facts.

120. On this phenomenon, see Leah Price, *What We Talk about When We Talk about Books* (New York: Basic Books, 2019).

121. For a thorough analysis, see Tim Wu, *The Attention Merchants: The Epic Scandal to Get Inside Our Heads* (New York: Knopf, 2016).

Credits

008, 092 *Portnoy's Complaint* by Philip Roth. Cover design by Paul Bacon. 011 *The Tin Drum* by Gunther Grass. Cover design by Gunter Grass. 012 *You Shall Know Them* by Vercors. Designer uncredited. 015 *Goodbye Columbus* by Philip Roth. Cover design by Paul Rand. 016, 082, 091 *Catch-22* by Joseph Heller. Cover design by Paul Bacon. 017 *Beyond the Pleasure Principle* by Sigmund Freud. Cover design by Herb Lubalin. 018 *The Last Tresilians* by J.I.M. Stewart. Cover photograph by David Larcher. 019 *Fraud* by David Rakoff. Cover design by Chip Kidd. 020 *How to Win Friends and Influence People* by Dale Carnegie. 021 *Ready to Riot* by Nathan Wright Jr. Design by Ronald Farber. 022 *Jaws* by Peter Benchley. Cover design by Paul Bacon and Wendell Minor. 023 *Sex Kitten* by Richard E. Geis. Cover design by Robert Bonfils. 024, 188 *Nineteen Eighty-Four* by George Orwell. Cover design by David Pearson. 025 *Self and Others* by R.D. Laing. Cover design by Germano Facetti. 026 *The Adventures of Augie March* by Saul Bellow. Designer uncredited. 027 *Mrs Dalloway* by Virginia Woolf. Cover painting: detail from a portrait of Virginia Woolf by Vanessa Bell. 028 *Of Mice and Men* by John Steinbeck. Designer uncredited. 029 *Light in August* by William Faulkner. Cover design by Alvin Lustig. 030 *Yoga* by Ernest Wood. 031 *Faster: The Acceleration of Just About Everything* by James Gleick. Cover design by Keenan. 032 *The Leaves of Time* by Neal Barrett, Jr.. Cover design by Mike Hinge. 033 *Three Tragedies: Blood Wedding, Yerma, Bernarda Alba* by Federico Garcia Lorca. Cover design by Alvin Lustig. 034 *The Move* by Georges Simenon. 035 *Tropic of Capricorn* by Henry Miller. Cover design by Guy Nicholls. 036, 092 *Rabbit, Run* by John Updike. 037, 192 *The New Testament* translated by Richmond Lattimore. Cover design by Chip Kidd. Photograph by Andres Serrano. 038 *No Exit* by Jean-Paul Sartre. Cover design by Jean Carlu. 039, 088, 090,12 *Pro dva kvadrata (Tale of 2 Squares: A Suprematist Tale in Six Constructions)* by El Lissitzky. Courtesy of the collection of Jane and Stephen Garmey. 040 *Zoya* by Danielle Steel. Type design by Dave Gatti. 041 *The Psychology of Communication* by George A. Miller. Cover design by Harada. 042 *Compass* by Mathias Énard. 043 *It* by Stephen King. 044 *Timepivot* by Brian N. Ball. Cover design by Tom Adams. 045 *Lolita* by Vladimr Nabokov. 046, 131 *To the Lighthouse* by Virginia Woolf. Cover design by Vanessa Bell. 047, 090 *A Farewell to Arms* by Ernest Hemingway. 048 *Crash* by J.G. Ballard. Cover design by Chris Foss. 049 *Story of O* by Pauline Réage. 052 *Madame Bovary* by Gustave Flaubert. Cover by Christopher Brand. 052 *Ibid*. Designer uncredited. 052 *Ibid*. Cover by Milton Glaser. 052 *Ibid*. Cover illustration by Lorin Thompson. 052 *Ibid*. Apple Books, cover design by Oliver Munday and Peter Mendelsund. 052 *Ibid*. 1st Edition. Designer uncredited. 053 *Ibid*. 054 *Lolita* by Vladimir Nabokov. 054 *Ibid*. 054 *Ibid*. Butterfly drawing by Vladimir Nabokov. 054 & 091 *Ibid*. 054 *Ibid*. 054 *Ibid*. Cover design by Mark Cohen. 054 *Ibid*. Cover design by Lothar Reher. 054 *Ibid*. Cover design by Carol Devine Carson. 054 *Ibid*. 054 *Ibid*. 054 *Lolita* by Vladimir Nabokov. 054 *Ibid*. 054 *Ibid*. 054 *Ibid*. Cover photograph by Walter Carone. 054

Ibid. 054 *Ibid*. 054 *Ibid*.. Cover design by Beverly Le Barrow. 054 *Ibid*. Cover design by Bruno Binosi. 054 *Ibid*. Cover photograph by Walter Carone. 054 *Ibid*. 054 *Ibid*. 054 *Ibid*. Cover photograph by Werner Rebhuhn. 057 *Gravity's Rainbow* by Thomas Pynchon. Cover design by Matt Broughton. 057 *Ibid*. Cover painting by John Holmes. 057 *Ibid*. Designer uncredited. 057 *Ibid*. Cover design by Marc Getter. 057 *Ibid*. 057 *Ibid*. Cover design by Melissa Jacoby. 057 *Ibid*. Cover design by Frank Miller. 057 *Ibid*. Cover design by Paul Burgess. 057 *Ibid*. Cover design by Yuku Kondo. 058 *Ibid*. Cover design by Peter Mendelsund. 062-063 *Compass* by Mathias Énard. Cover design by Peter Mendelsund. 065 *Are You a Bromide?* by Gelett Burgess/Library of Congress. 066 Second edition of *Leaves of Grass*, 1856 by Walt Whitman, with praise by Ralph Waldo Emerson on the spine. 067 *The Art of Distillation* by John French, 1651. 069 *Citizen*, by Claudia Rankine. Cover: "In the Hood" by David Hammons. 070, 071, 090 First edition of *The Great Gatsby* by F. Scott-Fitzgerald. Cover design by Francis Cugat. 072 *Watergate* by Thomas Mallon. Cover design by Paul Sahre. 072 *The Secret History* by Donna Tartt. Cover design by Barbara de Wilde and Chip Kidd. 073 *Killing the Buddha* by Jeff Sharlet and Peter Manseau. Cover design by Paul Sahre. 073 *Ashes* by Kenzo Kitakata. Cover design by Chip Kidd. 073 *Haunted* by Chuck Palahniuk. Cover design by Jeff Middleton and Rodrigo Corral. 074 *The Eternal Zero* by Naoki Hyakuta. Cover design by Peter Mendelsund. 074 *You May Also Like* by Tom Vanderbilt. Cover design by Peter Mendelsund. 074 *A Good Comb* by Muriel Spark. Cover design by Peter Mendelsund. 074 *A Life of Adventure and Delight* by Akhil Sharma. Cover design by Peter Mendelsund. 074 *Subliminal* by Leonard Mlodinow. Cover design by Peter Mendelsund. 074 *Invisible Cities* by Calvino. Cover design by Peter Mendelsund. 074 *The Fifty Year Sword* by Mark Z. Danieleski. Cover design by Peter Mendelsund. 075 *Girl Who Kicked the Hornet's Nest* by Stieg Larrson. Cover design by Peter Mendelsund. 075 *The Book of Disquiet: The Complete Edition* by Fernando Pessoa. Cover design by Peter Mendelsund. 075, 165 *Talulla Rising and The Last Werewolf* by Glen Duncan. Cover design by Peter Mendelsund. 075 *Censoring an Iranian Love Story* by Shahriar Mandanipour. Cover design by Peter Mendelsund. 075 *Stay, Illusion!* by Simon Critchley and Jamieson Webster. Cover design by Peter Mendelsund. 075 *The Village Under the Sea* by Mark Haddon. Cover design by Peter Mendelsund. 076 *Leave Cancelled* by Nicholas Monsarrat. Cover design by Paul Rand. 077 *The Corrections* by Jonathan Franzen. Cover design by Lynn Buckley. 077 *Grand Union* by Zadie Smith. Cover design by Jonathan Gray. 078 *In Cold Blood* by Truman Capote. Cover design by S. Neil Fujita. 079 *The White Album* by Joan Didion. Cover design by Robert Anthony. 080 *The Year of Magical Thinking* by Joan Didion. Cover design by Carol Devine Carson. 081 *The Rings of Saturn* by W.G. Sebald. Cover design by Peter Mendelsund. 082, 93 *Jurassic Park* by Michael Crichton. Cover design by Chip Kidd. 082 *Shogun* by James Clavell. Cover design by Paul Bacon. 082 *Infinite Jest* by

David Foster Wallace. Cover design by Steve Snider. 083 *Coma* by Robin Cook. Cover design by Paul Bacon. 084 *Satin Island* by Tom McCarthy. Cover design by Peter Mendelsund. 085 *Satin Island* by Tom McCarthy. Cover design by Peter Mendelsund. 085 *Satin Island* by Tom McCarthy. Cover design by Peter Mendelsund. 086 *The House of Leaves* by Mark Danielewski. Interior page designed by the author. 087 *Satin Island* by Tom McCarthy. Cover design by Peter Mendelsund. 090 *Friendship's Offering*. Courtesy of the Bodleian Library. 090 *The Yellow Book*. Cover design by Aubrey Beardsley. 090 *Are You a Bromide* by Gelett Burgess. 090 *The Great Gatsby* by F. Scott Fitzgerald. Cover design by Francis Cugat. 090 *Chéri* by Colette. Binding design by Rose Adler. 090 Cover of the first U.S. edition of *Ulysses* by James Joyce. Cover design by Ernst Reichl using a typeface designed by Paul Renner. 090 *The Vision; or Hell, Purgatory & Paradise of Dante Alighieri*. Worthing Co. Argyle Press printing and Bookbinding (1844). 090 *Hospital Sketches and Camp and Fireside Stories* by Louisa M. Alcott, with illustrations. Roberts Brothers (1883). 090, 96 *Four Plays* by Émile Augier. Published by Alfred A. Knopf. 090 *Home to Harlem* by Claude McKay. Cover design by Aaron Douglas. 090 *Moby Dick* by Herman Melville. Cover design by Rockwell Kent. 090 *A Farewell to Arms* by Ernest Hemingway. Original Penguin Books mechanical designed by Edward Young. 090 *Corsica and Napolean* by Ferdinand Gregorovius, translated by Eward Joy Morris. John E. Potter and Company (1855). 090 *Pro dva kvadrata (Tale of 2 Squares: A Suprematist Tale in Six Constructions)* by El Lissitzky. 091 *New Directions 10: In Prose & Poetry: An anthology of new writing*. Cover art by Lee Mullican. 091 *Ulysses* by James Joyce, Modern Library, 1940. Designer uncredited. 091 *Daisy Miller* by Henry James. Cover design by Robert Jonas. 091 *Illuminations* by Rimbaud. Cover design by Alvin Lustig. 091, 112 *The Catcher in the Rye* by J.D. Salinger. Cover design by James Avati. 091 *Lolita* by Vladimir Nabokov. Olympia Press (1995). 091 *The Printing of Books* by Holbrook Jackson. 091 *The Maltese Falcon* by Dashiell Hammett. Cover art by Leo Manso. 091 *The Wisdom of the Heart* by Henry Miller. Cover design by Alvin Lustig. 091 *The Decisive Moment*, photography by Henri Cartier Bresson. Cover design by Henri Matisse. 091, 157 *Prejudices: A Selection* by H.L. Mencken. Cover design by Paul Rand. 091, 274 *The Immoralist* by André Gide. Cover design by Antonio Frasconi. 091 *Designing a Book Jacket* by Peter Curl. 091 *Kill Me, Sweet* by Jess Wilcox. Cover painting by Lou Marchetti 091 *Le Modulor* by Le Corbusier. Cover design by Le Corbusier. 091, 101 *Ulysses* by James Joyce. Cover design by E. McKnight Kauffer. 091 *The Scarf* by Robert Bloch. Cover design by George Salter. 091, 149 *Atlas Shrugged* by Ayn Rand. Cover design by George Salter. 091, 156 *Invisible Man* by Ralph Ellison. Cover design by E. McKnight Kauffer. 092 *The Voyeur* by Alain Robbe-Grillet. Cover design by Roy Kuhlman. 092 *Lolita* by Vladimir Nabokov. Cover photograph by Bert Stern. 092, 113 *A Clockwork Orange* by Anthony Burgess. Cover design by David Pelham. 092 *Franz Kafka*, by Max Brod. Cover design by Leaonard Baskin. 092

by John Gall. 269 *The Lennon Play: In His own Write* by John Lennon, Adrienne Kennedy, Victor Spinetti. Cover design by Lawrence Ratzkin. 271 *The Brothers Karamazov* by Dostoevsky. 272 *The Thin Man* by Dashiell Hammett. Cover photograph by Peter Barbieri. 272 *The Voyeur* by Alain Robbe-Grillet. 272 *The Time Machine* by H.G. Wells. 272 *The Magic Mountain* by Thomas Mann. 274 *Stick Your Neck Out* by Mordecai Richler. Cover design by Lawrence Ratzkin. 274 *The Immoralist* by André Gide. Cover design by Antonio Frasconi. 274 *Wisdom of the Heart* by Henry Miller. Cover design Ivan Chermayeff. 275 *Deliverance* by James Dickey. Cover design by Paul Bacon Studios. 275 *Reunion & Reaction* by C. Vann Woodward. Cover design by Leonard Baskin. Typography by Edward Gorey. 275 *Brave New World* by Aldous Huxley. 275 *Invisible Man* by Ralph Ellison. Cover art by Ben Shahn. 275 *Moonraker* by Ian Fleming. Cover design devised by Fleming, completed by Kenneth Lewis. 275 *Hopscotch*, by Julio Cortazar. Cover design by George Salter.

Acknowledgments

Several individuals contributed to this project over the years: Beth Blum, Bill Brown, Vincent Brown, Glenda Carpio, Carol Devine Carson, Teju Cole, James F. English, Sarah McNally, John Gall, Henry Louis Gates, Jr., David Pearson, Jonathan Gray, Jamie Keenan, Gary Fisketjon, David Pelham, Jonathan Pelham, Janet Hansen, Kaitlin Ketchum, Annie Marino, Jane Chinn, Lisa Regul, Rachel Kushner, Chip Kidd, Chris Parris-Lamb, Günter Leypoldt, Deidre Lynch, Barbara Epler, Alison MacKeen, Helen Yentus, Sharon Marcus, Jesse McCarthy, Tom McCarthy, Eric White, Scott Musty, Claire Messud, Craig Mod, Oliver Munday, Kinohi Nishikawa, Catie Peters, Leah Price, J. D. Schnepf, John Stauffer, Jenny Wapner, James Wood, Lorin Stein, Jane Garmey, Erik Rieselbach, Glenn Horowitz, Jay McInerny, Jennifer Pouech, Paul Spella, Chloe Scheffe, the Smithsonian Institution, and all the book designers who have contributed down the decades to this great historical legacy. Thank you all.

Earlier portions of this book were published in *Public Books* and *ELH*. Thanks to the editors of those publications for permission to reprint.

Audiences at The Harvard Bookstore, Harvard University, The Heidelberg Center for American Studies, The Mahindra Humanities Center, The Netherlands School of Literary Studies, and Stanford University listened attentively and asked insightful questions.

This book was partially supported by funding from the Division of Humanities and the Faculty of Arts and Sciences at Harvard University. Thanks to deans Mike Smith, Robin Kelsey, and Heather Lantz for their support.

Index

All rights reserved.
Published in the United States by Ten Speed Press, an imprint of
Random House, a division of Penguin Random House LLC, New York.
www.tenspeed.com

Ten Speed Press and the Ten Speed Press colophon are registered
trademarks of Penguin Random House LLC.

Book cover credits are located on pages 282–285.

Publisher Attribution by Page Number
Altin Kitaplar Yayinevi: 54; Arkham House: 183; Beacon Press: 137;
Brandon Books: 156; Cassell & Company Ltd: 91; DK Gyldendal: 54;
Europa Editions: 210; Evergreen: 92, 156, 157; Faber and Faber: 91, 128,
129, 190; Fitzcarraldo Editions: 42, 93; Gallimard: 54, 265; Graywolf
Press: 69; Grove Press: 102, 165; HarperCollins: 90, 136, 146, 176, 180,
207; Hachette: 43, 82, 93, 138, 139, 144, 172, 173, 207, 272; Houghton
Mifflin Harcourt: 34, 93, 97, 114, 130, 144, 147, 233, 275; Il Saggiatore:
197; INDO Serambi: 54; Kawade Shobo Shinsha: 54; Lancer Books:
32, 183; Library of Congress: 65; Livre de Poche: 133; Macmillan: 37,
57, 77, 92, 93, 118, 142, 152, 156, 157, 173, 187, 192, 207, 261, 264; Michel
Lèvy Frères: 52; Midwood: 156; Monarch Books: 157; Mondadori: 54;
New Directions: 29, 33, 62, 63, 81, 90, 91, 102, 103, 156, 224, 225, 229,
274; Norstedts: 210; Olympia Press: 49, 54, 91, 195; Omega Boek: 45, 54;
Other: 15, 21, 23, 26, 35, 39, 53, 54, 58, 66, 67, 88, 90, 91, 93, 95, 99, 108,
120, 121, 122, 123, 124, 125, 126, 127, 132, 134, 135, 151, 156, 157, 158, 163,
168, 169, 179, 183, 187, 196, 206, 208, 210, 230, 243, 244, 245, 246, 247,
253, 254, 261, 262, 272; Panther: 48, 181, 183; Penguin Random House:
8, 11, 17, 18, 19, 22, 24, 25, 27, 28, 30, 31, 36, 38, 40, 41, 44, 46, 47, 52, 54,
57, 72, 73, 75, 76, 78, 80, 82, 83, 86, 87, 90, 91, 92, 93, 96, 100, 101, 102,
105, 106, 107, 109, 110, 111, 112, 113, 116, 117, 119, 130, 131, 140, 141, 143,
144, 145, 148, 149, 151, 155, 156, 157, 158, 160, 161, 162, 166, 167, 171, 172,
173, 174, 175, 179, 180, 182, 183, 188, 189, 191, 194, 195, 199, 202, 205,
206, 207, 208, 210, 214, 215, 216, 222, 223, 229, 263, 264, 268, 271, 272,
274, 275; Princeton Architectural Press: 93; Simon & Schuster: 12, 16,
20, 52, 70, 71, 79, 82, 90, 91, 92, 150, 151, 153, 154, 156, 157, 207, 264, 269,
274; Suhrkamp: 210; Text Publishing Company: 210; The Theosophical
Publishing House: 168; Thorndike Press: 77; Vertical: 73; Weidenfeld: 54;
Zone: 93

Library of Congress Cataloging-in-Publication Data is on file
with the publisher.

Hardcover ISBN: 978-0-399-58102-1
eBook ISBN: 978-0-399-58103-8

Printed in China

Design by Peter Mendelsund and Paul Spella

10 9 8 7 6 5 4 3 2

First Edition

David Alworth

is the author of *Site Reading: Fiction, Art, Social Form* (2016) and the editor of the Norton Critical Edition of *The Great Gatsby*. He has taught literature, media studies, and cultural history at University of Chicago and Harvard University.

Peter Mendelsund

is the author of the non-fiction works *What We See When We Read* (2014) and *Cover* (2014), and the novels *Same Same* (2018) and *The Delivery* (2020). He is the creative director of *The Atlantic*.